Live, Learn, Love:
With an Open Heart

Life Lessons on Cultivating Healthy & Meaningful Relationships

Teriece Cherell

Live, Learn, Love: With an Open Heart

ISBN: 978-0-578-21439-9

Unless otherwise indicated, Bible quotations are taken from The King James Version.

DEDICATION

THANKING ALMIGHTY GOD for allowing me to share this with you all. May you all live, learn and love your life and the people in it.

This book is dedicated to my grandmother, Maggie S. Reynolds who instilled in me a strong sense of faith, the importance of getting an education, being independent and following my dreams. Thank you for your love, wisdom, guidance, and the life lessons during the time we shared together. Thank you for keeping me straight and putting me in check when I needed it. I truly miss you and wish that you were here sharing in this moment. Yet I know that you are always with me as I carry you in my heart and sweet memories. I believe that you are smiling down proud of your Sweetie. I will never forget the lessons you have taught me. My better days are coming, I've kept my head to the skies. You are my guardian angel. Love you MawMaw.

To my daughter, Tiana who has taught me so many things about myself. I thank God for choosing me to be your mother. You have made me realize that it is not all about me. You have taught me to channel my inner child. You are the reason for everything that I strive to do. I hope you are as proud of me as I am of you. You can be, do and go wherever you choose. Just allow God to lead you, stay humble, have courage and never give up. Love you Tiana girl.

ACKNOWLEDGEMENTS

THANKING GOD FOR the opportunity to share part of my journey and for placing this purpose and passion inside of me. Thank you for creating me as I am. I appreciate and know who I am.

To my mother, Cheryl, thanks for your love and support. To my father, Terry (Peanut), thank you, and to my brother Gary, I am still the big little sister. To my baby girl Tiana, thanks for being my biggest fan and sharing me with others. To my Uncle Tyrone, thanks for always being there for me. I couldn't do this without any of you.

To all my family members and friends who've supported and encouraged me in any way. Special thanks to my sister girl Kita B. for your assistance and support along this journey. Thanks to The Wiltz Family who welcomed me and Tiana into their hearts and home years ago.

Special thanks to C.C. Harrison, this book would not have been possible without you. I thank God for your vision and allowing you to fulfill your purpose by helping me and so many others to discover our purpose. I pray He continues to bless and pour into your life as you pour into the lives of others. Thanks for helping me obtain my All Access badge.

Bishop Lester Love, Pastor Fran Love and the entire City of Love Church family, thank you for being there to see my growth. I also thank you both for your guidance, support and encouraging words. Additionally, I want to offer gratitude to Elders Johnetter Hall, Adrienne Davis, and Marie Carter for speaking into my life and encouraging me to be the woman whom God called me to be.

Shout out to Bianca and Gregory Jacques for your support, and many thanks to my Payne Memorial AME Church family, my first church home, for your love and support.

I would like to thank "The Quad" (Danika, Vanessa, Ana and Toya), the RBC family, Donna Lima of Corporate Connection, the officers and members of the Order of Eastern Stars, Prince Hall Affiliation, Louisiana Jurisdiction, District #1, and my chapter, Herman P. Bush #173.

Finally, thanks to all of you whom I have encountered on this journey. There are too many people to name, but you know who you are. Whether we realized it or not, our paths are all intertwined and connected. This is for you.

PREFACE

WHEN I FIRST DECIDED to write this book, I wasn't initially sure of what I would share with you. I knew that I had a story and I wanted to share it to encourage and inspire others. I thought about my personal journey and how it could help others to overcome some obstacles in life. I knew that it was going to highlight some parts of my life and the lessons that I have learned along the way. Both good and bad experiences came to mind and how they have all contributed to the individual that I am today.

Moreover, I often think of how everything is connected to my various relationships and the role they have ultimately played in my life. This book is designed for anyone who has loved, experienced loss or been hurt, but now want to heal. It is for those who seek that unconditional, authentic love we long to share with others. May you find the love you truly deserve and seek to reciprocate it to others. My prayer is that anyone reading this book can seek out God's plan and purpose for their lives. May they experience the true love that is within all of us and manifests itself without. May they allow the lessons and blessings of life to bring them closer in all of their relationships.

The title of this book was inspired by one of my favorite artists, India.Arie and the feelings invoked by listening to her album, *Testimony Vol.1: Life and Relationships.* As I listened to her songs, I thought of living a more simple life, and I remember how her songs made me feel. It made me both happy and sad. I wanted to laugh, cry, dance and scream all at the same time.

For years, I lived as I had until it got to the point where I could no longer ignore the signs. I needed to face the truths... *My Reality*. It was time to take back my power. The power that I, unbeknownst to me, freely relinquished... *The power of love*. Life has taught me so many things in my 33 years. During this time, I have lived, loved, lost and learned. I am not perfect, and neither is my life. Here is my journey, and I welcome you into my world. My heart is open to you.

FOREWORD

ON FORTUNATE OCCASIONS IN LIFE, we discover a breath of fresh air in someone who crosses our path. Someone filled with optimism, enthusiasm and a zeal for life, love and the pursuit of learning all they can to get better and to enrich the lives of others. This is what I have found in Teriece Cherell. She is a refreshing reminder of all that it means to evolve and follow the certain steps towards success.

Happiness is the pursuit of many; however, few are willing to sit at the feet of others to embrace the lessons that will surely lead to achieving worthy goals. Teriece is one who will, and in this book, she willingly shares her experiences and conveys to the reader the valuable life lessons she has learned. Although her life has not been free of adversity, she has endured and used obstacles as opportunities to emerge as a winner. She transparently tells her story to inspire us all.

Within this book, Teriece Cherell strides into another realm evolving into the product of all the experiences she has gained through relationships. She is just the example you need to realize that success is possible if you are willing to embrace an open heart, engage in life and build positive relationships with God, your family, your friends and your finances. As you read on, I hope you will discover her secrets to overcoming all in order to find peace, happiness and self-love as she has.

INTRODUCTION

"We learn something from everyone who passes through our lives. Some lessons are painful, some are painless... But all are priceless."
-Author unknown

THIS QUOTE SUMMARIZES how important a role relationships play in our lives and what we experience. Life has many lessons to teach, and through our relationships, we discover who we really are. Relationships are very crucial to the success or failure of every human being. Nothing and no one can exist alone in the world. All relationships are not created equal. Good and meaningful relationships bring out the best in us, while bad relationships can bring out the worst in us. However, they all bring out something that either we did not know existed or was just afraid to face. For example, we have all been through some relationships which we knew we should not have given a second thought. We knew that individual was not right for us, yet we were excited about the idea of him or her and the feelings they stirred within us at a specific time.

There were warning signs we chose to ignore for whatever reason. Maybe we did not want to be alone, were naive, easily deceived, or whatever the case was. There were moments when we wanted, needed and should have walked away, yet we did not for some reason or another. What makes you stay in an unhealthy relationship? What makes a relationship unhappy? What are the signs of an unhealthy relationship? Conversely, what are the most common elements of a truly loving relationship? How can healthy relationships positively affect our lives?

Even the relationships that hurt us are designed to teach us lessons. Throughout this book, we will explore and discuss the various types of relationships and the most common elements for fostering healthy, successful relationships. We will also discover how these relationships can contribute to our overall success and growth as individuals. It will help readers begin to see relationships for the blessings and lessons they teach. Readers will understand that when some relationships end, they make room for better, more mutually beneficial relationships later on down the road of life.

TABLE OF CONTENTS

SECTION 1

Living the Life

CHAPTER 1

Faith Is

"Faith is like Wi-Fi... It's invisible but it has the power to connect you to what you need."

SO, WHAT IS THIS THING CALLED FAITH? Why we do need to have faith? What does having faith do for us? Faith is believing that anything is possible. It is seeing things that cannot always be seen through our physical eyesight. For me, faith is believing that this book will be completed when it is meant to be. Faith is believing that it will bless those who read it. Faith is knowing that God's promises to me will be fulfilled. Faith is knowing that something is, and will be true. Faith can even make you do some things contrary to common sense. Faith is knowing without a doubt that whatever we believe and work towards, will be so. Faith is knowing that even when you lose someone or something, you still win.

There was a time when my faith wasn't as strong as it is now. One day I was on my lunch break sitting on the balcony, and as I read, *Can You Stand to Be Blessed* by well-known Pastor, author and speaker, Bishop TD Jakes, I felt overwhelmed but in a good way. It was as if a ton of bricks hit me. *What was I doing here*? I envisioned myself doing what I was purposed and being prepared to do. I felt that I had something to say and people should hear it. I had decent faith, but where had it gotten me so far. I had about as much faith as the person sitting next to me at church.

I am a work in progress, and I was just trying to get better in all aspects of my life. Isn't that the reason we attend church? To get better, to live a more Christ-like life? So why was I still here, in this space? Did I not know that God had more in store for me? Did I not believe that the best was yet to come? Did I not know that it was my time to reap the harvest? Yes, I knew all of these things, because I had faith. Faith in God, faith in myself, and even faith in some others to help me get where I needed. Life has a way of knocking us down and trying to keep us down. It has a way of making us feel as if we are less than who He created us to be.

"Faith is taking the first step even when you don't see the whole staircase".
- Rev Dr. Martin Luther King, Jr.

To have faith in God and His plans for our lives, means that we fully trust Him. Trusting in the Lord is not just a phrase, it is a call to action. It requires us to do something. When we trust God, we give it to Him and move on to something else. We don't worry, complain or fret over our burdens because our relationship with Him tells us that He will take care of us.

We know that fear and faith cannot dwell in the same space. Faith helps us to understand that everything happens for a reason, that everything has its time and place, and that dates determine destiny. Having a strong sense of faith is something that most Christians struggle with daily. It may sound easy, and we can easily quote various scriptures on it. Specifically, we recite *2 Corinthians 5:7…"For we walk by faith, not by sight."* We may also look to *Proverbs 3:5… "Trust in the Lord with all your heart and lean not unto your own understanding."*

All of this sounds good, and we know that hearing the Word of God builds our faith, but how many of us get stressed out and want to give up when "life happens" to us? You see, it's difficult to trust God when there is more month left than money, when you lose your job, or when you're living from paycheck to paycheck. When that man or woman leaves you and your children... How can you trust God or remain faithful to Him? We pray, but do we truly and fully submit to God? Do we wait on Him, or do we take matters into our own hands? Let's keep it real. You can fool your neighbor, you can even fool yourself, but you cannot fool God. Placing our relationship with Him first and building our faith will help us in relationships with others… Relationships with our family, our finances and our friends.

There can be no complete relationships without God because the ultimate relationship begins and ends with God. God is the Alpha and the Omega. My relationship with God and the building of my faith in Him have been strengthened. As I write this book, tears are falling down my eyes as I think about the goodness of God. He is so great, and we do not always deserve His grace and mercy; yet He gives it to us freely even when we disappoint or hurt Him, His people and fail to live a life pleasing in His sight. When we sin and do not ask for forgiveness, when we know better but don't do better, God is still good and faithful to us.

When I began to focus more on God and what He said, instead of what family or friends said, I began to see things more clearly. When you focus on God, you can tune out those distractions all around you. No, they don't disappear, but they are smaller because God's presence and position is now Bigger. You see, God is like the wind, you can't see Him, but you can feel His presence. If you're quiet enough, you can hear His voice speaking to you. When we place God first, our desires will align with His desires for our lives. We begin to experience life in its fullness. And then things happen suddenly, immediately, just like that. Doors open to us and opportunities arise that we didn't know existed. We have that All Access that C.C. speaks about. We get access to the next level, next dimension and next phase in our lives.

We all experience things in life that cause us to doubt ourselves and even God, but the fact is that we are still here, still standing. Sometimes we feel as though we've waited long enough for our turn, our big break, our breakthrough in life. Even during our waiting, we should know something is happening for us. God is working it out behind the scenes. I've learned to depend on God because He is my strength and He can do ALL things but fail. I find joy in knowing that God loves us despite our faults, flaws and failures. God has our backs, and we are His children! We NEVER have to question God's love, loyalty or faithfulness to us because He never changes! He is the same true God, yesterday, today and forevermore! Yes, there will be ups and downs, good and 'not so good' things in life, but we embrace them for the lessons and blessings that they teach us.

Looking deeper into my faith, I know that everyone was created by God in His image and likeness and for His purpose. We all have certain gifts we were born with...Gifts from God and gifts from the Holy Spirit. Frequently, I have confused myself with what I thought or wanted my purpose to be instead of consulting with God about what His purpose is for my life. As a result of this, I have spent precious time wandering aimlessly trying to figure out something I could not until I asked God, my Creator. I have not only frustrated myself but others in the process. Who else could know my purpose better than God himself who put me on this earth for this very reason? The purpose of my life is bigger and better than I initially thought.

You see, our purposes should be about more than just making money, being happy or achieving social status or wealth. Now do not get me wrong, all of these things are nice, but they cannot lead to the true fulfillment of purpose in life. Clearly stated, we can have all of these things, achieve success by the world's standards and still miss out on the purpose for which God placed us here.

Without God, life has no purpose. Without purpose, life has no meaning. God has placed us here to live a life with meaning. I cannot count how many times I wondered why I was placed on this earth? What am I supposed to be doing? What contribution could I make to this world? I have realized my purpose is bigger than me. Not so very long ago, I traveled down this same road of trying to figure it out... Knowing that I was here for a reason, but I just could not figure it out. Doing this, doing that, looking here, there and everywhere. Yet when I relinquished power to God, things started to fall in line for me. One of my favorite bible scriptures Matthew 6:33 states, *"But seek ye first the kingdom of God and His righteousness, and all these things shall be added unto you."* If we allow God's love, grace, wisdom, and strength to fill us, we will never feel alone, unloved or empty inside. So even though we cannot understand what's going on, we can trust God and know that "All things work together for the good of those who love God and are called according to His purpose."

This past summer, I attended The Purpose Driven Church Conference in Orange County, California. Many may be familiar with Rick Warren, author of the *Purpose Driven Life* and *Purpose Driven Church.* You may have read the story of how he traveled to California and founded Saddleback Church. Almost 40 years later, there are over 15 campuses in Southern California and another 4 campuses in other countries. Nothing happens in life by chance. Everything happens for a reason and has its specific time.

Therefore, it was no coincidence C.C. Harrison, one of my mentors asked me to speak about 'Discovering Your Purpose and Passion' during an upcoming seminar at her foundation, shortly after we attended this conference in late June. I was unsure how C.C. decided to ask me to speak, or if she already knew what the next monthly series would be before the trip. Maybe she was inspired by the trip and all that we had experienced at the Purpose Driven Church Conference. However, I do know that attending that conference had changed my life. I was fired up and ready to live in my purpose and passion, or at least re-evaluate what I thought it was. I wanted to get on the right track. It was also no coincidence that on the eve of my 33rd birthday, I was sitting on my balcony writing these pages.

Upon completion of a special class at my church, called *Discovering Your God-given Gifts*, I discovered that we are all driven by something or someone. There are many different reasons, circumstances or factors that may drive us. The most common factors that drive people are as follows: 1) ***Guilt*** which allows the past to control you. It causes us to run from regrets and hide from shame. Rick Warren frequently says, "We are products of our past, but we don't have to be prisoners of it." God's purpose is never limited by our past. 2) Some people are driven by ***Resentment***. We have been hurt, let down or disappointed by those we love and care about. Resentment can keep us from moving on hindering our spiritual progress. 3) Another factor is ***Fear*** which can hinder growth on all levels. This fear can cause us to miss out on life's opportunities by forcing us to play it safe at all costs. I believe that you now understand the power of passion.

When you are so passionate about something, you will think about it all the time. You will be willing to wake up early and sacrifice your sleep for it. Passion about something keeps you up late at night, wakes you up out of your sleep and has you inside on the weekends. Missing out on what others are doing. However, once you ask God, and He reveals your purpose to you; you do not have to validate or explain yourself to anyone. People begin to see things in you that you did not see in yourself. Therefore, having passion is important, because it can drive you each day to achieve what you want in life.

Knowing Our Purpose

Here is the mistake most of us make in discovering and pursuing our purpose. We look for people and things to give us meaning and value instead of living a life pleasing to God. My daily prayer is that I will lead a life pleasing in God's sight. Yes, that means that I have to become a new person in Christ.

When I was a little girl, I loved to read, speak, act and write. I started writing about my life, family and things I have experienced. I also wrote poetry, which I still do from time to time. Well as I grew older and other things occupied my space and time, I forgot about that book and did not finish it. Now, almost 20 years later, I am an author. Again, I say that God is good, and how amazing is He to always bring us back to where we are supposed to be. That book would have been good, but this one will be great. I have learned more, experienced more, shared more, lost more and even gained more. So now, I have more to speak about, and my experiences will help bless someone dealing with various issues I have encountered. I am saying this to say that many times people see things in you that you cannot or do not always see in yourself.

While I have always known I possess great potential, I have not always felt that way. Sometimes I do not feel like the "Most Ambitious Senior" Superlative elected by my high school classmates (Xavier Prep Class of 2003), yet I am. I am still Teriece, just not that same Teriece. You see, life had caused me to view myself a little differently now. I had gone through many experiences in life that seemed like an *'out-of-body'* experience. Where had that ambitious, talented, strong young woman gone? Was she lost or just on an extended vacation? I needed this woman to resurface as soon as possible and live up to her name.

Presently on my spiritual journey, there have been some recent personal developments. As I thought about who I am and who I want to become, I realized that I had to refocus and redefine some things in my life. As my pastor, Bishop Lester Love says, "The only thing better than a word from God is a confirming word from God." For the past few months, I had been thinking and doing some soul-searching. I can never forget the weekend right before my 33rd birthday. Bishop prophesied to me at our weekly Saturday morning prayer service, the Encounter Experience. What he told me would change my life more than he could ever know! It was as if God used him to call forth who I was meant to be!

In other words, it was as if the voice of God said, "Teriece Cherell come forth... You have been hiding and running for too long." The funny part was, I didn't even know that I was doing it. Let me explain. Prior to this day, most people knew me as "Hollywood", my nickname which encompassed a free-spirited, fun-loving, life of the party, cool, somewhat crazy and well-liked individual who adorned sunshades to all occasions. I would even wear them and keep them on during church.

I was frequently called upon to participate in various events, plays and several types of productions, and the truth of the matter was... As much as I liked attention and the spotlight, I did not like it at the same time. Some people thought I hid behind the shades for some reason or another. They were a part of my personality-*my favorite accessory*. They allowed me to be seen yet unseen at the same time. Isn't that what the celebrities do? They sometimes wear sunshades, so you cannot notice them. They try to hide behind this disguise, but most people still recognize them.

Some people figured it was a silly phase I would outgrow, and still others thought I was just crazy for wearing shades all the time. What is she trying to hide? Does she have a black eye? Has she had a long night and needs to cover her face? It is amazing what people make up or choose to believe, when they do not know the truth. It never really occurred to me what people thought about my wearing these shades until I received the confirmation from Bishop Love. And it's funny because these things were so far from the truth. There was another more serious side of me that only a few people had encountered.

On the contrary, I am a philosophical thinker--*an overthinker sometimes,* and I always like to process scenarios. I have learned how to rationalize situations, see the good in everyone and try to become a beacon of light and hope to others. Sometimes in life, you reach a point where you cannot take everyone along for the ride. When you are trying to live a life for God, you may lose some family members, friends and even parts of your old self. Yet I realized, this was a new season of my life. You see, God was doing a

Brand-New thing in me. I was excited, ready and willing to embrace this next level, but it wasn't going to be as Hollywood. It was going to be as the woman God created me to be, Teriece Cherell.

So it is with chapters in a book. As one chapter ends, so does another one begin. A new day, a new beginning, another chance, another sunrise, and another opportunity to attempt to live a life pleasing in His sight. Someone once said, "Are you living or are you just existing?" I began to ponder this question and frequently wondered about which category I fit.

CHAPTER 2

Family Matters

"Family....like branches on a tree, we all grow in different directions, yet our roots remain as one."
- Author unknown

IT IS IMPOSSIBLE TO SURVIVE without the relationships in our lives. We were designed that way. Whether we realize it or not, our earliest experiences with relationships come from our family. Some family relationships are good, some are great, while still others may not be so good. Yet these relationships lay the foundation and are the basis for all our future relationships.

My relationship with my immediate family is simple, complex, happy and sad all at the same time. Generally, when I think of the word *family*, I think of immediate family: parents, siblings and grandparents. However, a family is more than just those members who may reside under the same household. It also extends to our aunts, uncles, cousins and even those who enter our family by birth, marriage, or adoption.

Our most influential relationships can come from our families especially that of a parent and the child. As a parent, you provide for, protect, and you seek to instill certain morals and values into your children. You take care of business and do what is best for your family. As we are products of our parents, it is funny how we become like them in some form or fashion.

I was blessed to grow up in a two-parent household for a period of time. Both of my parents had good jobs, and we were considered part of the working middle-class. Yes, we lived in the C.J. Peete Housing Development, better known as the Magnolia Projects, but no one knew except those who really knew us. If we were considered poor, I did not know it at that time. It was not a place to be ashamed of, but something to say with pride. My brother and I attended Catholic schools for which my parents paid our tuition. This is not to say that we were better than other children in the neighborhood. Our parents just worked hard and wanted better for us. They made sacrifices to ensure we had what they did not have growing up.

My mother Cheryl was a hardworking, ambitious young woman. My relationship with my mother was pretty good. Although I've not yet revealed this to her, I saw her as some type of superwoman who made things happen for us. I didn't question where or how we were going to get what we wanted. I just told my parents, Cheryl and Terry, what I wanted and somehow, someway, it happened. We were exposed to traveling, taking family trips and other things at an early age. We also experienced the lives they wanted us to have. Growing up, I knew that my mother loved and cared for me.

Yet, there were times when the love seemed to be displayed differently towards my brother, Gary. As it can be with boys, my father was a little stricter on my brother. This led to an unforeseen sibling rivalry between my brother and me. He was a momma's boy and I was daddy's girl. So, as I grew older, our relationship became somewhat strained. Yet upon graduating from college, we began taking mother/ daughter cruises in September for my birthday. Even though our relationship has had its "ups and downs", she has always been there for me when I needed her. And still to this day, she is here to support me and provide assistance in her own way.

On the other hand, I was a daddy's girl at heart. As the youngest child and only girl, I was his little princess. I used to follow my daddy everywhere I could. We would go to the A.L. Davis Park, also known as Shakespeare Park, walk together as we followed the second line that passed uptown through the neighborhood. When I became older, we had our Father/Daughter dates on the weekends. We would sometimes catch the Freret Street bus to Canal Street. On those weekends, we did whatever I wanted to do. Sometimes we would go to the Joy Theatre to watch a movie. Other times we went to the Riverwalk where we could eat and then do a little shopping afterwards.

After my parents divorced, my father and I remained close. Yet as I got older, I began to notice some changes in him I had not noticed before. When I was away at college in Virginia, we would call each other and talk for hours. He called me *'Lil Juice'* because I always had some juicy news to report about someone or something that happened. As much as I cherished these times, there were some moments when I was very disappointed in him.

Disappointment, especially from those that we love can really hurt us in unimaginable ways. It can sometimes harden our hearts and minds. It can change the very dynamics of our relationships and how we view certain things in life. Although our relationship has been broken, I am willing to pick up the pieces and mend it. It is still there although it is not what it was once.

However, the good thing about some broken relationships is that they can be mended, healed and restored. I am no longer that little girl anymore. I am a woman with a child of my own, so I know and understand the importance of a parent/child relationship and how this relationship can affect us.

One of the strongest influences came from my paternal grandmother, Maggie affectionately called "MawMaw". I can remember being a little girl sitting in her lap, being held in her arms. She was the sweetest, most beautiful, generous, no nonsense woman that I knew. There was just something about being at MawMaw's house. As a little girl, I always felt the love, warmth and kindness while with her. There was no other place I'd rather be than my grandma's house.

As I grew older, my grandma's house became the meeting spot for my friends as we made our weekend plans. They knew that they would get a plate of good food, love and a life lesson. She didn't sugarcoat anything and would tell you off in a minute if it was necessary. Even when she put me in my place, I did not stay mad at her for long. I knew that it came from a place of genuine concern and love. She only wanted the best for me and saw some things in me that I did not see in myself. She wanted me to be the woman that God created me to be.

Although we would sometimes have our disagreements about things, I knew it was only because she wanted the best for me. She just wanted me to avoid some mistakes in life, but we all know experience is the best teacher. Sometimes we are just hard headed and have to learn about life in our own way and time. We have to get knocked down a few times, get up, dust ourselves off and move around again.

She was one of my biggest supporters and always took care of me, her baby. When I was sick or not feeling well, I knew that no one would take better care of me than my Grandma. As I talked to her and listened to those stories of old, I thanked God that He placed me in this family. As I grew older, all I wanted to do was make my grandmother proud of me. I was her 1st grandchild to graduate from college.

I remember being at the hospital when she passed away. It was a cool Sunday morning in December. December 23, 2012, to be exact, and I went to the 8am service at the City of Love Church. The family was called to the hospital the night before. As I stood in church singing with tears rolling down my face, I knew that it was only a matter of time before she left us. I had heard stories of how people on their deathbeds would recover and get better. Yet my strong faith in God believed that He could turn this situation around and restore my grandmother's health. I knew that it was possible but only if it was in His will. I attempted to prepare myself for the inevitable.

I thought about our last trip to Texas fleeing from Hurricane Isaac that past August. I thought about our last words and moments together. I thought of how she always ensured that her baby had a nice birthday, as she knew how I felt about my birthday. Flashbacks of all the things I didn't say or do for her came to mind. There was not much to regret, as I knew how much she loved me and vice versa.

The New Orleans Saints were playing the Dallas Cowboys in Dallas. My mom was cooking her famous pot of red beans for the game. I told her and my uncle that I was going to take a ride. I didn't want to tell them that I was really going to the hospital. My Uncle looked in my eyes and knew where I was going. He didn't want me to go alone so he rode to the hospital with me. We were the last two people at the hospital with my grandmother when she died. My Uncle stood there watching the game and me as I talked to my grandma.

As I watched her on that machine, her chest faintly moving up and down, I kissed her and thanked for everything she had done for me. I told her how much I loved her and that we would be alright. We were all we had at that moment, other than God. About 20 minutes later, she left us.

How devastating it is to deal with the death of a loved one, especially a close one. We feel many emotions ranging from sadness to grief to anger. We may even feel relieved and happy that they are no longer suffering. We hear things such as, *"time heals all wounds"*, or *"this too shall pass in time"*. Yet no one can determine how much or how little time is necessary for getting over the loss of a loved one, relationship, or some other devastating life event. The pain will lessen more and more until it fades away and becomes a distant memory. Prayer will get us through anything if we have faith in God and believe that everything happens for a reason.

During these difficult times, it is very important to have the support and love of family and friends. There are some family members that you can live with, and there are some that you just cannot live without. One such family member is my favorite Uncle Tyrone. I cannot live without him, yet I know one day I will have to do so. But until that time comes, he is stuck with me and Tiana. He is the best example of the true caliber of a man that I can offer as he stepped in as a young man to help raise his deceased, older brother's daughter. Not many people would have given up their lives at such a young age.

He has been a father figure to most of his nieces and nephews. He too has been one of my biggest supporters, always in my corner and cheering me on. Even when I did not always make the best decisions, he was on my side and encouraged me. He was never judgmental about the choices I made. He always believed in me and even in those moments when his faith may have faltered, we were able to talk about it. We've had many heart-to-heart talks over the years. Conversations that I could not or would not share with anyone else.

Unselfish, generous, faithful, helpful and dedicated to his family are a few words to describe him. These are some of the characteristics my future husband will possess. As much as I wanted to live my life, I just felt as if I couldn't disappoint him or my grandmother. Nothing hurt me more than when I felt as if I had disappointed either of them. It was as if a knife had cut me deep. Isn't it funny how certain people can have such an impact on you? These relationships have forever changed and shaped my life. I am the woman I am today mostly because of these early influences.

People always say that tragedies can either bring families together or tear them further apart. Both sayings are equally true, as I have witnessed them at different times in my life. During the writing of this book, I learned that my oldest brother, Tommye, had died. I did not sleep well at all during this time. Waking up early, going to bed late, my mind was all over the place. So many questions, yet not enough answers. I needed to know what happened to my brother. There was also something else that weighed heavy on my mind.

A few weeks prior to this unfortunate incident, my nephew reached out to me while I was at work. I told him that I would call back once I got settled at home. But life happens, and once I got off from work, I was too busy to return the phone call. Neither one of us called back, and the next month he was gone. Never to hear my voice again or vice versa. I think of what our last conversation would have been about. It was a trying time for my family, but the Lord gave us strength when we needed it most.

My middle brother Gary and I are 5 years apart. Gary and I had not traveled anywhere together alone, but there we were... Just the two of us. My mother joked that she sent two children to Virginia, and she wanted two to return home. Yet we knew that we would make this trip and bond like we had never bonded before. We had lost many relatives, but this was our oldest brother. This was a journey we would share together. We would cry and hold each other. This was actually the closest that I felt to my brother Gary in a long time. He may not have known it, but I looked up to him when I was a little girl. To him, I was the aggravating little sister who wanted to follow him around or be in his business. To me, he was my big brother who would fight and protect me if needed.

Although we argued, fussed and fought as siblings do, we loved each other in our own way. We were really all we had in terms of siblings. So, when he graduated from high school and went to the United States Marine Corps, I missed him. I would lay on the floor in my room listening to the radio. When certain songs came on the radio, I would cry to myself or write some poetry. I would never tell him this because I did not want him to think that I really cried over him. I mean, he was an *alright* big brother but not one for me to cry over like that.

Growing up as a member of a large family, we engaged in many events with extended family members. There were family cookouts, parties, trips or just family gatherings with food, fun and music. I was usually the baby of the group. I liked to be around my older female cousins who would comb my hair and take me out with them. Usually when we traveled with my Teedie Pat and her kids, I was the only girl with my brother and older male cousins. No one wanted a little girl around when they were trying to shoot their best shot at the young ladies or just be cool; so I traveled with my own friends, a good book, my baby doll and some David sunflower seeds.

While everyone may not be blessed enough to have a strong, familial influence, they may have a good relationship with others in their circle of influence including trusted family friends or those they may deem as significant. It may either be a mentor or a close relationship with a friend's parent.

My most significant relationship currently is with my daughter, Tiana. Many people may consider their greatest achievement to be such things as graduating from high school, college, getting married or having a great career. My greatest achievement is something quite simple, something that others may take for granted. My greatest achievement is becoming a mother. Outside of my relationship with God and my future spouse, my relationship with my child is the next most important relationship. There is no closer relationship than that of a mother to a child. For most people, having children brings out a side that they never knew existed. In other words, this motherhood thing is something very serious.

I never really understood how special mothers were until I became one myself embarking upon a lifelong journey and learning experience. I can remember the day when I discovered I was pregnant. From then on, I knew that my life would never be the same, so I began preparing for the day I would become a mother. This bond that is formed during pregnancy is unlike any other bond that I can imagine. All of the physical, emotional and hormonal changes were well worth it. As the time rapidly approached, I became anxious, excited and tired. Tired of waiting for my baby to come into the world. Then finally the long-awaited day came.

When I looked into the eyes of my baby girl, I knew that I loved her more than life itself. I knew that I had to be the best woman that I could be for us. I wanted to set a good example for her. I thank God every day for blessing me with such a healthy, happy, beautiful baby girl. Having someone else to care for totally changed my perspective in life. I had to become more mindful of my decisions, the company I kept and the things I did. Not that I was doing wrong, but I had to be even more careful than usual. Not only was I responsible for my life but for that of another person as well.

Motherhood is such a blessing. Every morning I wake up, I think of how I can be the best mother to my child. I want my child to be proud of me and for having me as a mother. I vow that my child would have everything I had and more. Yes, I make mistakes; and I don't always get it right, but I try my best. By God's grace and mercy, I manage to do it well.

As a parent, I make sacrifices for my child. I work hard so that she can have what she needs and some of what she wants. Because I want her to experience certain things, I may work longer hours or get another job for extra money. I may not go to lunch with my friends so that she can attend her play date with her friends. I may forgo my sale at Bath and Body Works so that she can have the special toy because her grades were great. These sacrifices are minimal because the rewards of seeing the smile on her face, joy in her heart and laughter in her voice are well worth it.

Tiana represents the best parts of me. She has parts of my personality coupled with bits of her own. I see so much of me in her, yet she is also different. I seek to instill in her the same values that were instilled in me as a little girl. I try to be the best example of a woman living out her dreams, remaining faithful to God and His promises, helping others and being humble. I want her to know how important she is to me. I don't want to look back and as she gets older, wonder where the time went. I want her to be strong and independent.

As parents, we try to protect our children from the harsh realities of life; and while we try, we cannot shield them from everything. Life just happens sometimes, and when it does, I will be right there for her with open arms, mind and heart. When I spend time with her, I always try to teach her about life, about me and about her relationship with others. I want her to know that people will sometimes do things to hurt her, but she has to love them, forgive them and move on.

So, what does it take to build a loving relationship after you've been hurt or betrayed by a family member? What does it take to move past the hurt and pain? My spiritual response would be to pray to God for guidance, healing and understanding of the situation. To recognize the lesson in it and move on with your life. More often than not, this is easier said than done. We tend to replay the situation over and over in our heads causing us to relive the hurt and pain all over again. On the other hand, the human side of us wants to hurt them like they hurt us, make them feel how we felt so they will think twice before they hurt anyone again. But the truth is, it takes many things such as time, prayer, patience, understanding and forgiveness.

This is why communication is so important to have in all types of relationships. It is not selfish to express yourself and let someone know that you were offended by something that was said or done to you. These feelings, when left unexpressed, lead to anger and resentment. Such matters should be approached in a calm, non-accusatory manner. Now the contradiction is this, some things are better left unsaid. People say, *"let sleeping dogs lie... Be careful when you wake them."*

Conversely, how many times have we allowed some relationships to end because of our pride or stubbornness? In cases like this, a simple yet sincere apology can mend the relationship if both parties are willing to bury the hatchet. The harsh reality is that life can be short, and we never know which day will be our last. We don't want to leave this earth with any regrets because of having some broken family relationships. No, we may not always like each other, or the things said or done to us; but we do love each other.

I'm not saying to let some family members make a fool of you, or constantly hurt you. Rather, I am saying to love them, pray for them and move on with your life. We can spend this time fostering those family relationships that bring peace, love and happiness in our lives. So, it is important to love our family members even if from a safe distance.

CHAPTER 3

Friends and Finances

"Good Friends are like stars, you don't always see them, but you know that they are there."

WE TEND TO THINK OF FAMILY as those who are related to us by birth, marriage or adoption. We think of friends as those people we've grown up with, whether in our neighborhoods or even a classmate. Yet some of our friends become closer than our family members, and those really good friends become our family. They love us, support us, encourage us and are there for all of the other moments in life. Real friends are those individuals whom we cannot imagine our lives without. They are there for the moments of joy, pain, sunshine and rain that happen in our lives.

A true friend is a gift to cherish from God. I have some friends whom I may not see or communicate with for weeks or even months at a time, but I never question their loyalty to our friendship. Life gets in the way and due to work, family, church and other obligations, we are sometimes unable to keep in contact as often as we would like. But when we can manage to catch up... whether we talk on the phone or hang out, it is like we have not missed a beat. Time has stood still, and we enjoy those moments of catching up with each other.

Moreover, friends can come into your life at any time. Some friends we may know for years, yet others we meet later in life throughout phases of good times and bad times. No matter when or how we met them, I believe true friends are gifts to us from God.

As many people as I know, I have very few people whom I actually call friends. My Uncle taught me to be careful with freely giving that title, because everyone I know may not be called my *friend.* The title *friend* is given to those who have earned it. When we think of a friend, we frequently think of someone with whom we grew up, attended the same school or lived in the same neighborhood for a long time. And while this can be true, there are some real friends whom I have met later on in life. Although time may not be a determining factor for us, they have proven their loyalty, have been there for important moments in my life, and have supported me.

I have also supported and been present for them sharing in their dreams, struggles and transitions in life. Sometimes we may not agree with each other. Just like family, friends may disagree, fuss, and not speak to each other for a while, but the love is always there. The best friendships are those in which we are able to express ourselves without judgment, and we move on pass any conflicts to remain in close-knit relationships.

Although I don't have any biological sisters, there are a few friends whom I consider as close as sisters. One such individual is Cynthia Brown whom I met during my high school years at Xavier Preparatory High School. Cynthia and

I have been friends ever since. We've had our fair share of disagreements, but we have always been there for each other throughout the years.

Marquita Boyle is another close friend of mine whom I would consider as a sisterly type. She is not a childhood friend or even a former classmate. We met later in life, but we discovered that we are kindred spirits. We are alike in many ways; yet we are still very different women. Our friendship is a testament to how God brings like-minded individuals together for a common cause. We started out as business associates, but we have developed a strong friendship and sister-girl bond. We've been there for each other and have had each other's backs since we met. Some people we just gravitate towards and have good instincts about. She is one of those people.

Isn't it amazing how God can place people in our lives? Conversely, He also removes people from our lives as well. Although we don't always know when we will gain or lose friendships, I am grateful for both scenarios.

I like to listen to my friends discuss anything they are dealing with and help them to find a solution if necessary. I frequently offer my advice and words of wisdom. Sometimes I truly believe that I have missed my calling in life. I should have been a counselor, a life coach or maybe even a psychiatrist. I usually pray with and for my friends. I provide some practical knowledge coupled with personal experience; and most of the time, they are receptive and agree with what I have said. Or they give it some thought and things work out alright for them. Yet it's funny how I can give good advice to others, but I do not follow my own advice.

How can I impart such good wisdom inherited from my grandmother to others, yet I cannot follow it to save myself? Of course, when you are on the outside looking in, you can see things one may not see from the inside. You can see things objectively as opposed to subjectively when it doesn't directly affect you. Yet as good as the advice I offered to them may have been, I did not always practice what I preached in all areas of my life. The two most common areas of discussion were relationships and finances. We would talk about many topics, but it always came back to the two topics: relationships and finances. I advised my friends that once we changed our mentality on relationships and finances, then things would change for us.

A Better Relationship with Finances

"Take responsibility for your finances or get used to taking orders for the rest of your life. You're either a master of money or a slave to it. Your choice."
- Robert Kiyosaki

The above quote from noted financial guru, Robert Kiyosaki brings back thoughts of when I was a slave to money, for those are dreaded words no one really wants to hear. It's funny how we never think about things like that. My relationship with money has had its ups and downs because the area of *finances* and I tend to have this love/hate relationship. As with most individuals, I love to make and spend money, but at times it seemed to hate me, which is why I thought it ran away from me. Looking back, I admittedly have not always been the best manager of my money.

As a young child, I was not really taught the importance of saving money. Of course, we received a weekly allowance growing up, I saved my money until I wanted something my parents would not buy. Since I had my own money, I could spend it on what I wanted. Once I had graduated from college and entered the workforce, my mentality was like that of most young adults: I'm going to make money to spend money. And while that is true, it should also include saving and investing money as well.

I had to learn this lesson the hard way time after time. I didn't have to live that way. Like most young people, I had made some poor decisions regarding the spending of money and other financial matters. Consequently, I had a poor relationship with money. How many times had I spent more than I saved? How many times had I spent money on things I didn't need? There were times when I miscalculated what was in the bank and had to pay unnecessary overdraft fees. I didn't have to live above my means, *'living from paycheck to paycheck'* as they say.

These things were the result of poor money management coupled with the lack of understanding of the true value of money. That's the difference between our American culture and some other cultures. In other cultures, they are taught not only how to make money, but also how to save, invest and even share it with their families and friends.

Regarding the generation of millennials, a culture of young earners… They know how to make money, but they tend to spend it on cars, clothes, jewelry and other things that make them look cool or rich. Mainly because they are not taught the importance of saving money and living below their means. There comes a point in time when you should want more out of life. Your personal choices reflect this new mentality and the relationship you will have with your money.

In recent years, money and I had reached an agreement. I was in control of it, it was not in control of me. Of course, we all want to have more money which allows us to do more things; and while some people may dream of being rich, I just want harmonic prosperity. If I wanted to attract more abundance in my finances, I would have to change my mindset. I wanted to be like the servant in Matthew 25:21, "*Well done, thou good and faithful servant: thou hast been faithful over a few things, I will make thee ruler over many things: enter thou into the joy of thy lord.*" How could the Lord bless me with more if I was not taking care of what I already had? It made perfect sense and was a proven principle.

So, once I changed my mentality of money and its value, things began to change. I began to view money as an investment for my family's future. To me, money has become a resource to be utilized to have greater access to certain things in life. I have begun to see it as a friend and not a foe. I have become a better manager of my money, and we treat each other well. Nevertheless, I know that God is the source; but the people He has placed in my life, coupled together with my gifts, talents and treasures are the resources.

We are taught to be good stewards of what God has given us. Every time we give our tithes and offerings at my church, The City of Love, we declare that we are so happy to give, grateful for what we have and generous in what we give.

Even when I was unable to give the amount requested, I gave something to support God's kingdom work; and in those moments when I gave out of lack, it came back to me in double or even triple portions. One week, I was blessed financially three days in a row. All I could say was thank you God and cry to myself. It is not about the amounts we give, but more about our level of consistency and our heart's intention. We should give with an attitude of gratitude.

SECTION 2

Learning the Lessons

Sometimes I Wonder

A Poem by Teriece Cherell

Sometimes I wonder what my life would be like if I had you
Would it be better or worse? Would I be happier or sad?
I'm not really sure because I've had you and not had you at the same time.
I have learned to love myself first and most and to be happy with myself.
I have learned that true happiness comes from within and must manifest itself without.
Sometimes I wonder what it would be to wake up to you everyday
To come home to you after a long day at work
To cook dinner for you and help you unwind
To kiss you at night before bed and in the morning when I wake up
To hear you whisper my name in those passion filled moments we have so often
Sometimes I wonder how it would feel to be a constant part of your life
To feel the love and affection from you
Sometimes I wonder if you can return my love and affection
Sometimes I wonder if you are the One for me
To be able to take away the pain and stress in your life
To hug and kiss you and let you know everything is alright.

Sometimes I wonder

CHAPTER 4

Choices, Chances, Changes

"Choices, Chances and Changes... You must make a choice to take a chance, or your life will never change."
-Zig Ziglar

THE ABOVE QUOTE is a profound statement offered by noted motivational speaker, Zig Ziglar. Within each of us, lies the power of choice also known as the power of everything. Every time God blesses us with another day, we make conscious decisions. We choose whether we are going to have good days or bad days. We choose where we live, work and play. We decide what we wear to work, how we style our hair, what we drive and what we eat. Every day we make choices when choosing our friends, deciding how we will spend our money, and selecting where we may travel for our vacation. We can choose our career paths, where our children attend school and how we will celebrate our religious beliefs.

Furthermore, we choose those people with whom we will experience life and interact within meaningful relationships. We choose how long we will stay within these relationships, and we even choose what we will or will not accept from our partners. Oftentimes we do not realize how powerful we are and how the choices we make today can affect us tomorrow and years to come.

Everyone reaches that pivotal redefining moment in their lives. It is at this moment when you realize you may be on the road to self-destruction. You cannot and will not survive if you do not make a change. You must make a choice to make a change in your life. Lisa Nichols, noted author and motivational speaker said, "You have to be your own rescue." No one else can do this for you. You cannot wait for someone else to change your life.

I discovered that the most dangerous person is the one who has a problem and may be in denial about it. At least those individuals who admit that they have problems can seek help. Three things that I have learned with dealing with any issue: You must ***acknowledge***, ***accept*** and ***adjust***. The hardest thing to do is acknowledge that you have a deficiency in a certain area of your life. There is something that isn't right… something off balance that has you feeling off track.

The following is my acknowledgement of what I felt. Here I am, 33 years old and living a decent life by some standards. I am a single parent with an MBA, a good job, and yet I didn't really feel as though I was where I wanted or needed to be in life. I knew I had great potential, and I was certainly meant to do something greater…Something bigger than what I had already done. I was born not only to contribute to my community but to the world. I was not living my best life at that moment.

But the question was, *why not?* What or who was stopping me? How did I allow this to happen? When did I miss out on what I knew belonged to me? What could I do to change these feelings? Then I had to look deeper to do some soul searching. The answers to these questions awakened something in my spirit that I knew all along, although it was painful and still shocked me. Whoever said the truth hurts knew what it meant.

Yes, the truth does hurt, and reality can be harsh; but I was the reason why I did not have those things I felt I should have at this time. I was not where I should be because of some decisions I had made. I chose to spend my money on things I did not really need. I chose to hang out with my friends, eat out at restaurants or get my hair and nails done. I chose to spend my time being busy as opposed to productive. I chose to engage in unhealthy relationships, even if for a period of time. In and of itself, there is nothing wrong with these things. Of course, we all deserve to enjoy life and treat ourselves sometimes, but when you are headed to another level in life, you are required to make sacrifices. I had to give up some things and make a commitment to do some things differently in order to have different results.

You see, I wanted more and better for both myself and my daughter. I talked a good game, but I was not initially doing anything about it. I would start off with great momentum and then come to a slow, rolling pace. I would sometimes procrastinate or make excuses for why I could or could not do this or that. I was usually busy, as I am active in several different ministries at church and the Order of the Eastern Stars, just to name a few. But one day I sat down and thought about these activities. The truth of the matter was, why was I part of all of these organizations? Was it my innate desire to belong to something greater than myself?

On a day off from work, I realized that there was a difference between being busy and being productive. Moreover, it has been said that broke people stay busy, and productive people make profits. So, I thought of all the things I could do to maximize my time and productivity level. There were some things that I needed to either take a break from or just curtail entirely.

As I cleaned my bedroom, I listened to the words of India.Arie's song, ***I Choose***:

"But today, I have the opportunity to choose
Here I am now looking at 30, and I got so much to say
Gotta get this off of my chest, I gotta let it go today
I was always too concerned about what everybody would think
But I can't live for everybody; I gotta live my life for me.
I've reached a fork in the road of my life where
'And I choose to be the best that I can be
I choose to be authentic in everything I do,
My past don't dictate who I am
I choose."

I realized that true power lies within us and the choices we make. Looking back, I realize that I have not always made the best choices in life. I did what I felt was right at the time. I dated the person I enjoyed being with at that moment. I dated the person who brought out a certain side or feeling in me. I did not always date with intent or even look towards the future. So here I am... Single, saved and enjoying life and the people in it. I am single because I am not yet married, and it's mainly by choice, because I know what I want and will not settle for anything else. I am single because I needed to focus more on my dreams, my life and the direction in which God was bringing me. Now I see that I wasted valuable time that I cannot get back. Yet I realize that each experience has helped shape me into the woman I am today.

All relationships do not lead down the same road. I've embraced the blessings and learned the lessons all these relationships have taught me. I've dated the wrong person at the wrong time. On the other hand, I've dated the right person at the wrong time, and I believe that my best is yet to come. The next relationship will be the best and the last one. It will be the right person at the right time. I only seek to control those factors within my control; and while we cannot control other people, we can control how we respond to circumstances.

No matter what hand life deals us, we can choose to play it out to the end. We do not have to throw in the towel when it looks as if we will not win. We can positively affect them, or we can let them adversely affect us. Sometimes we allow things and people to choose us; and then we get stuck in certain situations. Sometimes we may not realize how that one little choice, change of mindset or behavior can affect our lives.

"He created humanity at the beginning, and he left them to the power of their choices. [15] *If you choose to, you will keep the commandments, and keep faith out of goodwill.*
- Sirach 15:13-15 CEB

So, we are all on this journey called life. I say journey because life is symbolic of a roller coaster ride... Full of twists, turns, highs and lows. We are all on a journey headed somewhere before this earthly life comes to an end. Some of us reach our destination fully, some are still on the journey, and still others wander aimlessly with no destination in mind. I think of how detours, roadblocks and even setbacks in life can affect our journey. No matter where you are in life, or how off-track you may be, you can always get back on track. It is never too late to find your way in life.

Life has its challenges, but once they are overcome, you are back on the road to the life you want. How we live this life determines how and what we can look forward to in the next life. Life has a funny way of teaching us things. It can be a cruel yet real teacher. If we pay close attention, we can learn a lot about ourselves, those around us and life in general; but we must be willing to live, learn and grow. There is something that we can take with us if we are open to receive it. Life teaches us lessons we cannot leave behind; yet life is what we make of it. It may be whatever we want it to be based upon our decisions, actions and reactions to situations.

If we make good choices, life can be good; but if we make bad choices, life can be *'not so good'*. As ugly as life can get on occasions, it is always worth living, for there is a new day coming. Each day is different and should be treated as such because each day is a gift from God... Another chance to serve and please God... Another chance to be happy, to make better choices, to love and to laugh... Another day to smile, to cry, to learn, to grow and to just live our best lives.

As I reflect and evaluate my life, I see it for what it is. I choose to accept it for what it is; however, I know that there is always room to grow and make it better. I can be, do and have exactly what I want as long as I *"Seek ye first the kingdom of God and His Righteousness and all these things will be added to me."* If we follow our heads, listen to our hearts and use the tools God has given us, things will be just fine. No, every day will not be a good day, but it will be embraced for what it is.

Many times, we feel discouraged or defeated when things do not work out the way we hoped they would. We begin to question and doubt ourselves and our decisions. We may even question God and what He has allowed, but there are no excuses to be made. I believe that when we know better, we should do better. Ignorance can only be used as an excuse until it is no longer an excuse.

"People come into your life for a reason, season or lifetime."

There are three different categories of people we encounter in our lifetimes. According to Michelle Ventor, *"People come into your life for a reason, season or lifetime."* As I pondered this statement, I thought of some people who had entered my life and were now gone or either still present.

Those individuals who come into our lives for a particular *reason* are there to help us fill a need we've expressed. In other words, they see a need and fill that need. They are sent from heaven to serve a specific purpose, which can be related to either something spiritual, physical or emotional. And once that particular purpose is fulfilled, the relationship comes to an end. We must learn to enjoy the time spent and appreciate the reasons God placed them in our lives.

The next set of individuals fit into the *seasonal category*. These individuals come into our lives during our seasons of transformation, change or growth. We have approached another phase in life where we can learn or share with others. They may have taught us about life or ourselves. These individuals bring us important things such as new life and love, joy in our hearts, or laughter to our souls. It is a great, indescribable feeling... One that we don't want to end. Sometimes it may feel too good to be true. And it is exactly that, both good and true, but only for a season.

One particular relationship comes to mind for this category. I was at a point where I needed to just focus on me and my child. I didn't want to start over again or just go through the motions. As I prepared to embrace my season of singleness, he came along. This was the answer to my unrequested prayer or either the answer to a long-forgotten prayer. We were exactly what we needed at that time. We enjoyed the time spent together and we brought something new to each other's lives. I frequently joked that I was *'just what the doctor ordered'* for him. You see, I represented that different, exciting element that he was missing in his life... *The Hollywood Factor*. Our relationship was different from his previous relationship. I was considered outgoing, bold, adventurous and funny. He was the quiet, soft-spoken, nice and very creative individual who had seemingly forgotten how to enjoy life and its teachable moments. He had gotten stuck into a comfortable routine of much work with little play. He needed and wanted to feel the love and appreciation that he had been lacking for a while.

Looking back, I realize that I was there to help him lead a more balanced life. He was there to support me, encourage me and teach me how to lead a slower paced life. He taught me how to enjoy simplicity and actively engage in necessary self-care. And as the time changed, so did the seasons in our lives. It seemed as quickly as he had entered my life, he exited stage right for a long break. He is currently still on that break waiting until his next scene towards the end.

I believe that the *lifetime category* is the best category of all. These individuals teach us important lessons and we must carry them with us throughout life. These lessons often outlive the person or even the relationships, as we will never forget what we learned from them. We are meant to learn the lessons, love the individuals who taught them, and practice these lessons in other relationships in our lives.

The problem most of us make is trying to place the wrong people in the wrong categories. We try to force those seasonal people placed in our lives into the *lifetime category,* but they are not meant to be. That is why these relationships do not work or last long enough. They are only meant for a specific reason or season in our lives, and once this purpose is satisfied, the relationships either declines or makes a turn for the worse. Either things change, or the individuals change in some way. But the truth is, neither person may have changed at all. They just stopped trying to force it to work and realized it was over. Seldom do we recognize these particular relationships for what they are meant to be. At this point, I am reminded of songwriter, Betty Wright's famous song, *No Pain, No Gain.*

'No Pain, No Gain'

"But love is a flower that needs the sun and the rain
A little bit of pleasure's worth a whole lot of pain
If you learn this secret, how to forgive
A longer and better life you'll live....
Anything worth having, is worth working for
and waiting for."

This verse is one of my favorite parts of the song, and I agree wholeheartedly with this statement. We all know that our relationships require work, sacrifice, commitment, honesty and a whole lot more. However, there is a difference between working on a relationship and forcing it to work. They may appear to have the same elements, but trust me, you will know when something is being forced. It will not feel good, it will not feel right, and this is when we begin to hurt each other and ourselves.

Arguments will arise over silly, trivial matters for no reason. Little things will begin to agitate you, and the very things that drew you to each other may threaten to tear you apart. In the beginning, he loved your ambition, creativity and independence, now he says you are too ambitious and thinks you're better than others. You loved his willingness to compromise and please you, now you wish he was a little more aggressive, decisive and manly.

More on choices

Just as we choose to stay in relationships, we can choose to leave those relationships that are unhealthy and not beneficial to us. We know when relationships are not really good for us. There were warning signs we choose to ignore, for whatever reason. Maybe we did not want to be alone, were naive, easily deceived or gave the benefit of doubt to that individual. There were moments when we wanted, needed and should have walked away, yet we did not for some reason or another. Why do we choose to stay in an unhealthy relationship? What makes the relationship unhappy? What are the signs of an unhealthy relationship?

An unhealthy relationship is one in which there is no growth and no life. All living things are meant to grow, and when things cannot grow, they began to decay and eventually die. The individuals involved in this type of relationship have decided that it was not worth the time, the work or investments needed to sustain it. This relationship is full of arguments with one partner receiving all the attention, as the relationship is often one-sided. The other person may feel as though he or she may be in a relationship by himself or herself.

Sometimes we stay in these relationships because we are comfortable with them, we have a history with these individuals, or because we have children involved. We may feel as though we cannot do better or find anyone else. None of these scenarios are good, valid reasons for staying in unhealthy and unhappy relationships. I believe that we use these excuses because we are afraid of the unknown world waiting outside of the relationship. Moreover, we are afraid to start over, we are afraid of what people will say or think, or we are afraid to seek out happiness in other aspects of life.

It is said that there is no such thing as a perfect relationship, I both agree and disagree with this statement. Yes, no one is perfect, and neither will all relationships be flawless. We are all guilty of making mistakes and bad decisions in our relationships. Yet I do believe that there is a relationship that is perfect for each of us. It may not work for our friends or family, but it can work for us.

Sam Keen said, "*We come to love not by finding a perfect person, but by learning to see an imperfect person perfectly.*"

Even the most successful relationships are not free of adversity. These individuals may argue, disagree or breakup for a period of time. The difference between healthy and unhealthy relationships is how these individuals chose to engage in conflict resolution. Those individuals in healthy relationships choose to address their issues, seek counseling, or whatever it takes to get through the situation. They believe that this relationship is a blessing from God. They choose to embrace and protect it as they are committed to keeping their relationship strong, by any means necessary.

CHAPTER 5

Commitment to Cultivating Relationships

"A true relationship is someone who accepts your past, supports your present, loves you and encourages your future."
-Unknown

BEFORE I BEGIN TO ADDRESS the importance of fostering healthy, loving relationships, it is necessary to define the word relationship. According to dictionary.com, a relationship is a connection between two or more people that shows how they may feel and behave towards each other. In other words, a relationship is any form of connection, association or affiliation with someone else. Relationships can take on many forms. The most common types of relationships fall into these four basic categories: familial, platonic, romantic, professional or casual. Some relationships are healthy, loving, and beneficial to all parties involved. Others may be unhealthy or harmful to one or both people involved. Yet they are all relevant and necessary to our existence. They are either lessons or blessings. Furthermore, relationships can teach us about life, ourselves, and others.

Relationships are crucial to the success or failure of every human being, for it is impossible to survive without relationships. We were not designed that way. So, what does a healthy, happy relationship look like? How does it make you feel? What are some factors that lead to these relationships? No matter which type of relationships you engage in, there are several principal factors which should be present in all relationships.

These factors when combined, lead to successful, healthy relationships. I have listed several of the most popular:

Communication
Respect
Trust/Honesty
Compromise/Sacrifice
Commitment/Loyalty
Support
Common Values
Forgiveness

While this list may not be all-inclusive, these elements are some of the best ingredients for fostering happy, successful, healthy and long-lasting relationships. Research shows that these elements are the keys that unlock the door to experiencing all that a healthy relationship offers. When they are present, you may feel loved, empowered, beautiful and ready to embrace the world. Knowing this, we can choose to have healthy, successful relationships. Once we know what we want and don't want, we can make better choices and avoid the idea of settling in our relationships.

Having healthy, meaningful relationships is as essential to us as the air we breathe. Relationships can be as simple or as complex as we make them or allow them to be! Wouldn't life be so much easier if we had a relationship manual? A proven, time-sensitive "how-to" guide that encourages healthy behaviors which lead to many happy, successful relationships. The world would be a better place to live. And while there are numerous books written on this subject, many people don't have the time to read about relationships when life is happening to and around us daily.

The reality is that most of us have learned about relationships through trial and error. While all relationships are not created equally, they are all vital to our happiness, health and lives. I love being in healthy, mutually beneficial relationships. Not just one-sided relationships where it seems as if it's one person benefiting from it. Relationships are beautiful flowers that must be cultivated and watered by time, love, attention and even transformation; yet one of my greatest fears of being in a relationship is that I never want to lose myself.

Sometimes we can get so caught up in others and doing what they want, that we can forget about ourselves and what makes us happy. Usually things are great in the beginning. If you have ever been in a budding, romantic relationship, you can attest that it's like feeling butterflies in your stomach when you meet someone new. You text all day, talk all night and cannot wait to see each other. You are anxious, excited and indifferent all at the same time. You feel like a little child with a crush.

After a while, you get to know each other better, and the initial excitement slowly wears off. You may realize that this person is not really who you once thought he or she was. This can be a good or bad thing... It just depends on the individuals involved. They can be even more wonderful than you imagined or not as wonderful, but take the time necessary to cultivate the relationship.

The Queen of Soul, Aretha Franklin, had a hit song entitled *Respect.* It is still one of my all-time favorite female anthems because we all want respect, but what exactly is respect? Is it something automatically offered in relationships, or is it something earned? When I initially think of the word respect, I think of paying attention to the other person and understanding the needs of the relationship. Respect is something that must be earned and cultivated as well since respect may come on different levels and phases in life. I have noticed that respect also comes in different forms. It is important to communicate with your partner exactly what respect means to you. Respect goes a long way in how you treat others and how you allow others to treat you. In order for you to respect others, you must respect yourself and know what it looks and feels like.

As a child in my parents' house, I had to respect and honor their rules. In other words, I did what I was told and expected to do while I was living there. When I grew older, so did my understanding of the term respect. My parents and grandparents taught me to be a respectable young lady. I did not cuss, wear clothing that was too short or revealing, and I tried to avoid those certain behaviors that would make me the target of someone else's disrespect. Sometimes women can be disrespected for wearing certain types of clothing or behaving in unbecoming ways. Respect is a *'give and take'*.

I was taught that in order to get respect, you must first give it. It is a relatively simple concept yet some of us fail at it sometimes. There are different levels of respect and it can be shown in different ways. For an example, when someone else is talking you should remain quiet and give her or him your undivided attention.

In business settings, you must respect your employer and what they expect. You must respect the rules and procedures of time, the dress code, expectations, and work ethic. You must respect the culture of the job if you are to remain successful in your position. You must respect also authority and follow the proper chain of command. Similarly, the employer should learn to respect your individuality and trust that you both have made the right decision to be there.

Another essential component of a strong, healthy relationship is trust. Trust goes beyond just words, thoughts, and deeds. Trust is one of those things hard to obtain but easy to lose. Everything in life relates to trust. Trusting both ourselves and others whether it relates to work or play. It is more than what we can see or hear. It is also those things that we do not see or hear. Trust is similar to faith, it just has to be there. Trust takes time to develop and yet one false move, word, or action can shake the very foundations of that relationship. I say that if I cannot trust someone, then I cannot and will not deal with that individual on any level. Trust can be tricky, as we may trust people just because we are family or friends. We may trust them because we think we know them or vice versa. Yet when trust is violated from someone close to us, it can be devastating.

Trust can make or break any type of relationship, whether personal, professional or familial. Just as there are various types of relationships, there are different levels of trust. Within romantic relationships, we trust that our partners have our best interests at heart. We trust that they would not intentionally hurt us, and we trust ourselves as well. There are some people we can trust with everything, some people which may be trusted with only certain things and some which may not be trusted at all. We should definitely stay away from this third category of individuals.

In a previous, romantic relationship, trust became a constant issue for me. It became one of those situations where I could not trust anything that came out of his mouth. For instance, he may have said he was going to the store. Based on previous experience, thoughts of where he was going before or after the store came to mind. How long was this store run going to take? Who was he talking to on the way to the store? This mistrust became so much to bear, and I realized how crazy this situation was becoming.

Let's face it, we've all been in relationships where trust was an issue. There were some things done or said that made us question how honest our partner was, especially about certain matters such as cheating or finances. You may have searched through the cell phone, wallet or purse looking for signs of infidelity. I too am guilty of this type of behavior. I looked through my partner's phone as I suspected he had been unfaithful or untruthful regarding something or someone.

And we all know the saying…'*Seek and you shall find*'. When I finally confirmed what I believed to be true, what was I going to do? Was I going to address the issue with him? Was I going to use this as ammunition for the future? Was I going to call the female and question her? Was I just going to ignore it and move on? All of these questions, yet there was only one answer: I had to make a choice, whether good or bad, about my continued role in this relationship.

Yes, it was as simple as that, making a choice; but what would I choose to do? Choosing to do anything other than leave would give him the idea that I really cared, that I was like the other females he encountered in the past. But I was unlike any of them. I was different, and I knew it. I was not going back and forth with him or her, so I made the best decision for me. I removed myself from this relationship.

Afterwards, I thought about what trust meant to me. How can I trust someone else if I did not trust myself? I trusted myself enough to know what I wanted and needed in my relationships. And this was not what I wanted, in any way. Looking back, I feel somewhat silly now. I mean, was it really that serious? If I cannot trust a person, then I choose not to deal with him or her on any level.

Compromise is also very important in maintaining our healthy relationships. It is not just always about you and what you want but about your partner and children as well. Things may not always go as you want them to go. For example, you may have to compromise on your upcoming movie and dinner date. You select the movie, and your partner chooses the restaurant; or you can take turns. If you do not compromise your beliefs or values, then we can understand when compromise in relationships is necessary. Sometimes, as they say, you may *'go along to get along'*, and that is all right. Just make sure that you are not doing anything that you may regret later, or anything that makes you feel uncomfortable.

I believe sacrifice goes with compromise. Just remember that as equal as we may like to be, there will be one partner who seems to sacrifice more than the other. As long as the same partner is not the sacrificial lamb, things should be all right. I believe it just depends upon the level of sacrifice and the reason for it. As a parent, I often make sacrifices for my child on a constant basis. I sacrifice my time, finances, and sometimes even sleep to make sure things are good with her.

Commitment and loyalty work together in relationships. You must remain committed to both your partner and yourself. Additionally, you must be committed to learning and growing both individually and together as your relationship changes over time. As with everything else in life, this takes some time and effort. When you are committed to someone or something, you are devoted and dedicated to furthering that cause, which in this case, is your relationship.

Consequently, that means you should do whatever it takes outside of hurting yourself or others. When you are committed to something and someone, it is such a great feeling. And when you know that person is as committed to you that's an even better feeling. It is important to be dedicated and loyal to ourselves. When we are committed to someone special, we can express how important they are, and we show our support to them.

Another element of a healthy relationship is support. Support comes in a variety of forms, but what does giving support really indicate? Frequently we are guilty of not knowing how to support our partners, friends, or family during certain times in life. Think of a time when you either did not support a family member, friend, romantic partner or vice versa. Support comes in various forms and can be either be financial, emotional, mental, a listening ear or a helping hand.

Many of us want support from our family and friends, but we are unable to articulate exactly what kind of support we need. We want them to support our dreams and goals. It may be as simple as just allowing space and time to think about some things. It may be supporting our events with a physical presence, or it may be a thought or prayer offered on our behalf. Support from others may allow us some free time by having our partners, friends or family members to take the kids out for ice cream, help a little more around the house, or just being there in whatever capacity is needed...Even getting up with me at 3am while I write this book.

We want others to support our places of business, and we often speak of people not supporting us. Young entrepreneurs generally relate support to finances. Whether we realize it or not, support may be as simple as just *'liking'* or *'sharing'* a post on social media (on Facebook or Instagram), referring someone to a particular place of business, helping to clean up, passing out flyers or just listening to you speak of your dreams and goals. The key is asking for support and being able to communicate what is needed. The genuine people who are in your life will support in whatever way they can.

Forgiveness is another important element of a relationship. Forgiveness is not a one-way street. You must first forgive yourself and then you must forgive the individual who hurt you. You must allow yourself to heal and not blame yourself for what did or did not happen in your relationship. You must forgive the person who hurt you and release the power of you. We've all been hurt in some form or fashion, and we've maybe hurt others in the past. Forgiveness allows us to move past the hurt and pain.

Lewis B. Smedes said, *"To forgive is to set a prisoner free, and that prisoner was you."* When we hold grudges and do not forgive those who have hurt us, we stop ourselves from growing and experiencing full lives. While we're still living in anger over what happened, the other party has moved on with their lives. Once we forgive both them and ourselves, we are free from the shackles of bondage.

These shackles are sometimes forced on us by unfortunate events in which we do not allow forgiveness. As previously stated above, having healthy and meaningful relationships is as essential as the air we breathe. Relationships can be as simple or as complex as we make them or allow them to be!

The Power of Connection

During various seasons of my life, God has placed certain individuals there for specific reasons. You see, God has a way of doing things and moves in His own way and time. He will place unexpected people in our lives at the most unexpected times. Some may have started out as casual acquaintances, some may start as possible business associates and even some as complete strangers. Yet the invaluable lessons that we learn from these individuals are priceless. Whether we realize it or not, it is all part of God's plan for us. Being connected to the right person at the right time in the right season makes all the difference in the world.

Everything has to be in alignment in order for it to work out perfectly. If you connect with the right person at the wrong time, you may miss out on the opportunity. If you connect with the wrong person at the right time, things still will not work out. But if you can connect with the right person at the right time, you begin to accomplish things you never even thought was possible. When you are connected to the right person, you can access those things and people previously inaccessible to you. I emphasize the right time because if you are in a season where you are not receptive to those people whom God has placed in your life, you will miss the next bus, plane or train headed your way!

Being connected to one of my mentors, C.C. Harrison at this time has allowed me to write this book. Of course, I could have written it at another time in my life; however, this is the time that it was meant to be. When we first sat down, and I told her that I wanted to write a book, she replied, *"Let's do it."* In that moment, I felt so many emotions: happy, eager, afraid, excited, encouraged and inspired. She asked me if I had a title and if I knew the subject matter of the book. She was pleasantly surprised when I told her my title, presented a tentative chapter outline, and even provided a description of what I wanted to address in this book. She immediately said, "Your book is about relationships." As I pondered this, I realized that she was absolutely right! All these experiences and lessons were based on those various relationships developed and fostered throughout my life. Like most people, there have been both good and bad, happy and sad times in my life. And I have survived them all, even the bleakest of those relationships.

She taught me that *'Accountability plus action equals access'*. When you hold yourself accountable to a process and follow through, it can open doors you never knew existed. I am so grateful and indebted to her. Just being a part of her organization, The All Access Foundation, Inc. has opened doors that I only dreamed of! Doors are our pathways to the next level of our lives. As one door closes, another door opens inviting us into even greater experiences. These doors often connect us with individuals whom we must meet on our journey.

I have several stories of connections, but I will only share a few to illustrate how God works. On the Saturday morning of my initial book cover photoshoot, I had an early hair appointment with my stylist. While waiting to get my hair done, several other women were there as well. You know how it is when a group of women get together. We were just having good, casual conversation about life, love, and celebrating a recent engagement of one of the hair stylists.

During the conversation, I shared part of my message entitled "Level Up" that I ministered at a recent Wednesday night bible study at my church. There was one woman who seemed really interested in the conversation. We were all talking, but like me, she had a special voice that commanded attention. There was also something familiar about her. The more we communicated, the more we discovered about each other. She asked my name, and I told her my birth name. I also provided my nickname, *'Hollywood'* just in case she knew me by that name. While she did not recognize me by either name, she stated that she remembered my voice. We seemed to recognize each other's face and voices, but we could not initially pinpoint from where. So here we were trying to think about how we could possibly know each other. Then it hit her, she worked at my dentist's office, but it was not just that. We had been in each other's company before. Maybe we shared a mutual friend or had worked in the same building. Whatever it was, there was no denying that God had brought us together for such a time as this.

Sabria began to speak into my life and tell me how I was no longer *'Hollywood'*. The funny thing is, she told me a few things she could not have known. She had no idea that some of the things she said to me, I had shared in my first sermon, "Level Up". I invited her to check out the message. As she sat and listened to it, she kept shaking her head and smiling at me. She advised me to beware of people who either cannot see or accept my change, my new being. Sometimes people have a way of keeping us in a box of who we used to be, as they want us to remain the person that we once were.

2 Corinthians 5:17 states, "*Therefore if any man be in Christ, he is a new creature: old things are passed away; behold, all things are become new.*" Most people knew me as *'Hollywood'*, but I am now Teriece Cherell in the Lord's eyes. When your name is changed, you are changed, healed, deliv-

ered from those things of old. You cannot do the same things you did before your change. Your flesh dies, and your spirit begins to live and shine bright.

Just from that brief conversation, we knew that we had been connected only by God's design. Sabria and I not only connected on a spiritual level but future business ventures as well. God is very intentional, and it was no chance encounter that we were both at the salon that day and time. This was the beginning of a mutually beneficial relationship. Here we were, complete strangers a few minutes ago, and now we were talking like old friends. It's funny how you can meet some people, and they instantly know that you are special. She did not know anything about me, but she knew that I had something to share, that I was different, and that God was doing something in my life. She encouraged me to continue to allow God to use me.

I am not here to brag, boast or even toot my own horn. You just never know who is watching you. People I did not even think knew me, had been watching me. I often speak about people seeing things in us that we cannot often see in ourselves. I will share with you what I mean. I've attended The City of Love Church in New Orleans for over 11 years. My pastor, Bishop Love recently spoke about the *'It'* factor we possess. Some people just have *'It'*, and nothing you say or do can take it away. Just accept it, acknowledge it and flow in it. When God has chosen you and shines His light about you, all you can do is sit back and let Him work in and through you.

Again, God places certain people in our lives at different times. Often times we may believe that it is by chance or coincidence; but God is very intentional and purposeful in His plans. So, it was no coincidence that I joined the Order of Eastern Stars, the day after my Grandmother had a fall that would prove fatal. God knew I would need some more positive, older women in my life, so there was also no coincidence that I joined a chapter that had mostly older women in it. Honestly, I am just realizing this right now. Looking back over my life, I realize everything was predestined and had to happen just the way it did. It was all part of my journey to where I am now... The journey back to Me. I sometimes wonder about things that happen in life. Does my presence or absence stop certain things from happening a certain way? In other words, would the same things happen, and I fail to be there to witness it? Or would something totally different happen from what I have witnessed?

Furthermore, as a member of the Order of Eastern Stars, I have met great individuals who have encouraged and counseled me along this journey. They either saw me as a daughter, sister or even a younger friend and assisted in any way they could. I've met many individuals who have welcomed me and my daughter into their hearts and homes. Almost every path I've walked in life has connected me with someone who has played a part in my story. Too often we don't appreciate these little parts of the puzzle; but we should remember that every piece of the puzzle is important and vital to the complete picture.

You never know who you will meet and how the connections we make today can affect our future. Just think about how many potential acquaintances we may meet on a daily basis. In the coffeeshop, walking down the street or even while riding in the elevator at work. Yet we miss out on it because we have our cell phones pressed to our ears or in our hands.

I have also been blessed by the associations made in the various workplaces as well. One such connection was with Donna, from Corporate Connection Recruiting and Staffing. She saw my strong work ethic, intellect, character and the skills I could offer an employer. During a period of unemployment, I worked on various assignments, mostly legal and administrative through the company. She promised to keep me working until she found a great home for me, and she kept that promise until I walked into the doors of Republic Business Credit.

I am usually one of the youngest people at my workplace, I tend to gravitate towards the more tenured, experienced coworkers. Some people have just taken a natural liking to me. I always put my best foot forward, and I go above and beyond the job description. I realize that jobs are not all-inclusive and that there should be no job above or beneath me.

Danika, Vanessa and Ana were the first three ladies whom I met when I entered the doors of Republic Business Credit. From the very beginning, they saw something in me and believed that I would be an asset not only to their respective teams but to the company. They offered guidance, wise counsel and assistance whenever needed. Vanessa frequently said to "Work the position you want, not the position you are currently in." So, I asked questions, went the extra mile, and inquired about the other pieces to the puzzle. As this was an unfamiliar industry to me, I wanted to know how everything fit into the bigger scheme of things.

After about 6 months, another position became available for which I was a candidate for promotion. It was in May 2017, and Bishop Love preached a sermon titled, '*It's Already Yours*'. He spoke about how the things we wanted were already ours if we believed it was so. I remember thinking that the interview was May 5th and that the number 5 represents favor. I knew I had favor with God, so I prayed, praised and prepared myself for this position. After a few weeks, I hadn't heard anything else about the position. Just before I went to ask about the status, I was offered my first promotion with the company.

I say this to say that when someone sees something special in you and shares that with you, just listen and pay attention. Sometimes we need friendly reminders of how good we are, for we are created in God's image and likeness. Sometimes we need to hear that we are doing a good job and receive appreciation for such things. Although we should not do things for the purpose of recognition, it does feel good when our hard work and efforts are noticed.

CHAPTER 6

Communication is the Key

"Communication to a relationship is like oxygen to life. Without it, it dies." Tony Gaskins

ONE OF THE MOST IMPORTANT factors in any relationship is communication. Communication can take on various forms: written, verbal, non-verbal and visual. Of these four, the more common form relating to humans are written, verbal and nonverbal. All forms are vitally important and may either positively or negatively affect any relationship. Do not underestimate the power of eye contact, hand gestures, facial expressions or a simple touch. Many times, our body language can communicate our interest in someone or something, or the lack thereof. We must be mindful of the signals our bodies send to others, especially during disagreements.

There are many good factors which positively affect the communication process, yet it is important to know there are also bad factors of communication. Destructive behaviors such as pride, arrogance, selfishness or stubbornness can lead to the downfall of our relationships. How many times have we allowed pride to enter into our hearts or minds to the detriment of our relationships? We were too proud to apologize, admit our mistakes or take responsibility for our actions. We may have played the blame game called *'catch back-get back'* or whatever games we felt like playing at the time. How many times have we been in disagreements with family or friends? We rolled our eyes, turned our heads, breathed deeply or even walked away. We were dismissive towards the other person because we did not want to listen to what he or she was saying, seemingly unconcerned and unbothered by their feelings. Even if there was a reason for this behavior, we do not realize how our actions affected the other person.

During a conversation with a friend, he commented the following: "Hurt people hurt people." This statement caused me to think of those few times when I may have intentionally or unintentionally hurt someone because of a past hurt I experienced. Sometimes we may not even realize how our actions, thoughts or deeds have hurt someone else. We say whatever is on our minds because we want them to know how we feel. We want them to feel our pain, yet we never stop to consider how the other person may feel about the situation. While I believe in expressing myself, I also acknowledge that some things are better left unsaid. We must learn when to say something and when to just breathe and let it go. Christians would say, *"Let go and let God."*

Most relationship experts strongly agree that communication is the key that unlocks the door to healthy and meaningful relationships. As simple as communication may seem, it is more than just talking and listening. It also entails the nonverbal clues we unconsciously give to others. Communication may be tricky because there is the possibility of having your thoughts and feelings misinterpreted or misunderstood by the other party. How many times have you expressed yourself only for the other person to entirely miss the point you were trying to make? You said one thing, but they either heard something different or interpreted it in a way other than what you intended.

When discussing personal or business matters, I strongly recommend face-to-face communication. Even when using written forms of communication such as emails, text messages or letters, it is easy to misinterpret the tone of the sender. It's funny how I can "hear" so much in a text message. When I read certain messages, it's like I can hear the person saying it, and I base my response on that. It is also important to give eye contact to the speaker. This is a sign of mutual respect and ensures the person knows that you are paying attention and showing interest in his or her feelings. Things such as texting, talking on the phone or watching television while someone else is speaking can be mistaken for disinterest or unconcern for what a person is saying.

A popular quote by Stephen R. Covey says, *"Most people do not listen with the intent to understand; they listen with the intent to reply."* I remember the first time I heard this quote. I was at work, and one of my coworkers was talking to someone about it. It brought back to mind previous situations in which I was quick to respond before the other person even finished speaking. This is something which most of us are guilty, and we do not even recognize it.

It is important to think before we respond or react to things. Often, we allow our emotions to affect our common sense, and this is when we may say or do things, we later regret. We tend to think with our hearts and not our minds. A while back, my pastor, Bishop Love preached a sermon on this subject. He said the heart was never meant to be followed, and I thought this was interesting because we all may know the saying...'*Follow Your Heart*', so this statement surprised me. I too have followed my heart, or so I thought at certain times.

They say your heart will not lead you wrong. Yet following our hearts has undoubtedly caused many of us some pain in our lives. This pain was manifested by the love that we may have shared in an unhealthy relationship. We may have thought we loved a person, so we allowed certain things we would never have allowed to happen.

Communication is one of the tools we must master in order to ensure success in all relationships. Effective communication is a skill that requires practice, time, attention and focus which is again, the main components of any relationship. We must practice effective communication with others, so we can have healthy successful relationships.

SECTION 3

Loving the Legacy

CHAPTER 7

Time Is of the Essence

"To everything there is a season, and a time to every purpose under the heaven. A time to be born, and a time to die; a time to plant, and a time to pluck up that which is planted; A time to kill, and a time to heal; a time to break down, and a time to build up."
Ecclesiastes 3:1-3 KJV

I HAVE ALWAYS had this strange fascination with time. There are many clichés relating to time and its effect on people and situations. Growing up, the clichés were: *'Time is on your side'*, *'Time is filled with swift transition'*, *'Time waits for no one'* and many other phrases we have all heard regarding the concept of time. Many of us wait for the *right time* to do certain things, but is there ever a right time? If everyone waited on the perfect time to act or go places, many people would leave this world as unfulfilled beings. Nothing would ever get done. Yet what is time?

Time is simply a unit of measure used to determine the action, process or condition of which something exists or happens. As I have matured in life, my understanding of time has changed. I try not to have a predetermined amount of time for this or that to happen. I strive to live more in the moment and not base everything on time. Yet when I think about the various seasons in my life and the things I have experienced, I have to acknowledge that time is very important.

When you start a new job, there is a training period which may last several weeks to ensure success on the job. Consequently, it takes time to learn a new skill, job or position. This type of on-the-job training may be practical, intense, and very hands on. Well, it works pretty much the same way in developing relationships of any kind. You must take the time to get to know the other person, their likes, dislikes, goals, dreams and fears. This cannot be done in a week, month or even a year.

Really good relationships are lifelong commitments. That means years of constantly learning, living and growing both individually and together. As you grow and evolve in your life, so should your relationships. The time it takes to build a healthy, solid relationship is necessary. Time is very important, and the amount of time spent developing the relationship is evident and marked by how well it progresses. Relationships are like precious flowers, as they require time, attention and nurturing from all individuals involved. What you put into it is basically what you can expect to get out of it. Nothing more and certainly nothing less. This requires talking, spending time together, and finding a healthy balance of time spent both together and apart.

While I seek to focus less on the time frame, I do not throw all caution to the wind. Not too long ago, I met a nice guy who was just coming out of a relationship. He was unhappy and had made up his mind that it was over and through. I was there as a friend with a listening ear and a firm shoulder upon which he could lean...An adviser of sorts. I informed him to take time for himself and not to rush into another relationship. Yet it seemed about a month or so later, we were in a relationship of some kind. We began talking on the phone more, hanging out and before anyone realized what happened, we were the new couple. Now do not get me wrong, nothing is wrong with that. Yet, this young man was not ready to be in another relationship. He didn't allow himself time to refresh, revive or refocus himself. We went with the flow because things felt good, right and natural.

I asked him if we were doing too much, too soon. He responded, "No" and asked who determines how soon and how fast our pace should be. He felt things were fine, and that we should continue to go with the flow. He did not feel as if anything was rushed or forced because it just felt natural. Yet it surprised me less than four weeks later. We both questioned what happened to us and how we used to be. Once you gain momentum in a new relationship, it is hard to slow down without losing something in the process. How could we go back and change things without losing feelings for each other? How could we start over and not take away what we had?

Nevertheless, we realized that while we could not go back, we could move forward at a pace comfortable for both parties. Just as our feelings had grown at this point, they could continue to grow if we allowed. Although it was impossible to change the past, we could make present changes possibly leading to the future success of our relationship. It is extremely easy to meet someone and get caught up in the time. Especially if they represent the qualities you desire in a partner. When they say and do the right things, you feel complete. Nevertheless, it is important to allow time for self-reflection, to breathe again, to learn yourself and appreciate your own company.

Time is very important and necessary in all stages of life. Many times, when we deal with the loss of relationships, we may not allow ourselves enough time to heal and grow. We say that we will take time; yet after a short period of time, we move on to the next best thing. We hop on the next bus or train seemingly headed in our direction only to realize that our stop was completely missed. The bus just kept on going headed down the path of destruction. We are often guilty of saying one thing and doing another thing completely opposite of what we intended. We say that we will take our time and get to know each other first, but when the feeling is right, we just jump right in.

However, it is vital that we take the necessary time to get to know ourselves. We need to experience life, love, and learn what we truly want and need from a relationship. Take as much time as needed in order to do what is best for us. Time is necessary in the foundation of building strong relationships.

There are also moments in life when we realize that what we thought was the right thing to do turned out to be a disaster. It could have been the right thing for that time. Even still, it may have been the right thing done at the wrong time. Hindsight is 20/20, they say; and oftentimes we realize things after they have happened. We think of what we want versus what we need in our lives. We want to be with him or her, but that may be not part of God's plan for us. Do we even really know what we need at that time? We think that we are helping the situation or person, but in actuality, our good intentions may do more harm than good.

For instance, in a previous relationship, my partner seemed a little distant and unlike himself, so I offered some time and space to get himself together. I thought that I was being an understanding mate, doing a good deed. You must be careful when offering time or space as this can either work for you or against you. Previous experience has taught me the less time you spend together, the less you communicate, unless you express yourself in another way. Either way you must accept, acknowledge and adjust yourself accordingly. We all need some time with ourselves to refocus, refresh, renew our minds, hearts and bodies.

Effective time management is crucial to the health of our relationships, no matter which category it may fall into our lives. In today's society, everything is competing for our precious, limited time. Our faith, our families, our relationships, and our jobs require time. We sometimes struggle to find a healthy balance so that we can avoid feeling as though we have neglected someone or something. It is important to set boundaries and give time to those things most important to us.

Too often we make time for everyone except ourselves. It is necessary for our physical and mental health and wellness to find regular time to spend with ourselves. This time allows for some much-needed self-care as well as a chance to miss our loved ones. It is said that you cannot miss what you never had. While I agree with this saying, it is equally true that absence makes the heart grow fonder. Spending time away from family and friends can lead to a deeper appreciation of these important relationships. Taking time to experience life and focus on our passions are important to the survival of our relationships.

We must also incorporate time for our families and spouses as well. Too much or too little time can prove disastrous. Setting aside scheduled time for self, our spouses and other relationships are very important. Although the time spent with each entity may not be equal, just make sure that time is cherished and appreciated. In other words, be present in the moment. Family time is family time, and when those events outside of our control arise, we can deal with them later.

CHAPTER 8

True to Me

AS A CHILD, my kindergarten graduation song was, Whitney Houston's, *'The Greatest Love of All'*. The words of the song are:

"The greatest love of all is happening to me
I found the greatest love of all inside of me
The greatest love of all is easy to achieve
Learning to love yourself is the greatest love of all."

As much as I love this song, I believe that the greatest love of all is the love of God. Secondly, there is self love. Self-love is real love. Before you can love others, you must first love yourself. Of course, you love yourself, and there is no one that loves you more than you. But what does it mean to really love yourself? What does it entail? When we truly love ourselves, we began to see ourselves as God sees us. You know that you are created in His image and likeness. You now understand and believe that your imperfections are what makes you perfect. You acknowledge your scars, bumps, bruises and you no longer try to hide them. You realize that each one has a story to tell. They are all relevant and vital to the man or woman you are today. You must know who you are and where you're going in life.

Do you know who you are? I mean who you really are? Not the person whom people think you are, not the person you think you are, and certainly not the individual you portray. I am referring to the person God created you to be. That man or woman who knows his or her purpose, stands unwavering in his faith and beliefs, ready to conquer the world! How well do you know yourself? I mean, honestly how well would you rate knowing yourself on a scale of 1 to 10? No matter how well we think we know ourselves, there is only one person who knows us more and better, and that is the Almighty God.

While I have always loved myself, there was a time when I did not always like myself. I did not like myself because of some past decisions I made. Sometimes I did not like the way I walked or talked. Yet as contradictory as it sounds, I have always loved myself and been confident in my talents and abilities. Knowing myself and my worth is all part of the process. One thing I have learned throughout my journey is to always be true to myself. I have learned to love myself first and most and to be happy with myself. I have learned that true happiness comes from within and has to manifest itself without.

When I think of being true to myself, several things come to my mind. I think of my personal beliefs and values, morals, honesty, what is and what is not acceptable to me. I always believe in being completely authentic and unapologetically me. I have learned to know, accept and appreciate who I am, along with my strengths, weaknesses, and past limitations. Discovering my purpose and passion while allowing myself to flow in it is what it's all about. Being true to myself means living life on my own terms, not based on someone else's standards but by the standards of God and what He placed inside of me.

Author and spiritualist, Don Miguel Ruiz says, "*Be impeccable with your word. Speak with integrity. Say only what you mean. Avoid using the word to speak against yourself or to gossip about others. Use the power of your word in the direction of truth and love.*"

In this quote, he expertly sums up what being true to yourself means. When we are true to ourselves, we cannot help but to be true to others.

While I can fool everyone else, there are two people whom I cannot fool: God and myself. He made me in my innermost parts and formed me in my mother's womb. He knows the good, the bad and the ugly about each of us; yet He still loves us unconditionally. There is no place we can go to hide from God. While we may run away some people or things, we cannot run and hide from God. Just think about it, this amazing God knows EVERYTHING... Even those things that others may not know about us. It is reassuring yet scary at times.

I believe most of us want to be known yet unknown at the same time. In the real world, most times we can choose what we want or don't want others to know about us. However, that does not work with the Almighty God. He possesses ALL knowledge of everyone. Hiding from God is like trying to play the game of Hide and Seek when you're hiding in front of the person who is supposed to find you. It seems crazy, and it just does not work like that.

While most of us may think we are running from God or what He has called us to do, the truth of the matter is, we are only running away from ourselves. But what we fail to realize is that there is no hiding place from God. God already knows what was going to happen before it even happens. So, the sooner we realize running from God is impossible, the better off we will be. Then we can realize that we are only wasting time, our talents and resources. You see life has a way of bringing us back full circle to where we were meant to be; and we are exactly where we are meant to be at this time. I have learned to appreciate my current state in life. No, I am not where I should be or used to be, but I am where I am meant to be at this time.

It's funny how when tragedy strikes, we talk about the person as though they were perfect or would do no wrong… *"He wasn't that type of person… I would've never thought she would have done that."* Yet we don't really know these people as well as we think. And how can we truly know someone else when we may not really know ourselves. *"Never say never"* is how the saying goes, because we never know how we will react in the heat of the moment, when tragedy strikes, when we are hurt, when love calls our name or when passion turns into pain. Life, pain and love itself can cause us to behave outside of our character. It may cause us to say, do and behave as individuals that we don't even recognize in the mirror.

One of the hardest lessons I have learned in life is that sometimes love doesn't love us back. When I went through my last breakup, I had to encourage myself and reaffirm my self-love. I knew my worth and what I deserved in a relationship. I knew better, I wanted better and I deserved better. I told myself over and over again that I loved myself first and most, after God of course. I mean how can I love someone else when I don't know how to love myself the right way? How could I be an example of the kind of love I wanted, needed and deserved? How could I obtain this form of love and desire? I decided to date myself and treat myself the way I wanted to be treated so I would know how it felt when that person came around. I needed time to heal before I jumped into another relationship.

So, I went places by myself and learned to enjoy my own company. I learned to enjoy those moments of solitude, whether it was practicing meditation or just some personal reflection time. I enjoyed being home, lying in bed, watching tv or reading a book. Of course, I loved to be around people having fun, being the life of the party. You know that person that loves to have a good time... the one not afraid to dance by herself. When others watch, they wish they could be like her, so carefree and just dancing to the beat of her own drum. That is me. But I needed to spend some quality time getting to know me and what I liked. I mean, I knew myself; but I didn't really know myself.

I was always busy, but I wasn't always productive in my busy state. Then I realized there is a difference between being busy and being productive. Several times a week, I had something to do after work. Whether it was a meeting at church, mime practice, OES meeting, credit event, or dance practice for my daughter. It seemed like there was never any time for me to just rest, relax and unwind. I loved to be outdoors and getting into something. I was the one who had to attend every event I was invited to, even if only to show my face for a short period of time.

Sometimes, I had to attend several events in one day, and while it seemed fun and had me feeling semi-important, I knew it was becoming too much for me. One day something was brought to my attention which caused me to re-evaluate some things in my life. Was I running away from something? Was it really necessary to be that busy? What was the purpose of doing all of these things?

As I thought about it, all of this running around made me tired, interfered with my personal time with God, and it took time away from my precious daughter. I also wasn't getting as much rest as I should. It was my 7-year-old daughter, Tiana, who said, "Not another meeting tonight Mom", as she gave me my weekly schedule of events. She has her own personality, so she said this in a joking manner. But it was far from a laughing matter. My daughter was very serious about this. The next statement stirred something within my soul, as she said, "you don't spend enough time with me because you're always going to a meeting or talking on the phone." Soon she walked out of the room in a dramatic manner. You had to see her theatrics because she truly gets her drama from her Mama, but as I watched her walk away, I thought about the truth of what she had said. I had to find a healthy balance for everything I had or either remove myself from some of those things. I wanted to incorporate all of those things that were considered important to me. I would do a process of elimination and release those things and individuals that were consuming my time without providing a return on my investment. If it was not adding to my life or it was not a mutually beneficial relationship, it had to go. I was going to have a liquidation sale, similar to what I see on the television commercials. They advertise that everything must go. I was reminded of this and began to visualize what and who would soon be leaving this scene.

As I looked deeper into myself and became a better person, things that used to bother me didn't affect me much anymore. I accept where I am, acknowledged where I have been, and I now embrace where I am headed. I am on another level now, and I choose to use my time more effectively. I seek to take things less personally and see things and people for what they are. You see, there comes a time when we outgrow some people and vice versa. You realize that you have little in common with them. Even the things that you did have in common are not enough to sustain a beneficial relationship.

I realize that I have more important things to do, think and become before my journey is over. Before I will allow myself to be in an uncomfortable atmosphere with certain people who pretend to care about me, I choose not to engage in those activities. I do not go where I'm not invited or feel unwelcomed. I don't harbor any hard feelings about it because I have matured in life. I choose to focus my attention and effort on achieving my goals, spending time with people who genuinely care about me and want to see me get better.

I strive more on being a better parent to my daughter. I will be there when she needs me, teaching her lessons that she will not forget, and showing her the strength of a woman. I am learning to appreciate the little things in life... The air, the sun, the sky, clouds, rain, sunset and the light that shines through me. I am learning to enjoy solitude and my own company. I am learning how to make more time for myself and to do what makes me happy.

Love in Relationships

"The best and most beautiful things in the world cannot be seen or even touched- they must be felt with the heart." - Helen Keller

Love is a beautiful feeling especially when shared with the right person and when the feeling is mutual. When some of those elements mentioned in Chapter 5 are present, healthy and successful relationships are created. Just think about it... Being with someone who adores, encourages, supports you and believes in your dreams. Teddy Pendergrass said it like this:

"It's so good loving somebody
and that somebody loves you back.
To love and be loved in return, is the only thing that
my heart desires."

Just listening to this song puts me in a mental zone. It allows me to travel to that relationship where I shared that feeling. I believe that romantic relationships are the best and require the most work and time. When you first meet a person, you are attracted to the physical being. She is simply beautiful or fine, or he is handsome and has a nice body. Don't get me wrong, nothing is wrong with it. Let's be honest with ourselves and each other. Of course, we all want to be with someone in which a mutual, physical attraction is shared. It is frequently said that *'beauty is in the eye of the beholder'*. We see beautiful women with men to which we probably wouldn't have given a second thought. Similarly, we see handsome, well-groomed men and say things like, "How did she get with him?"

During initial conversations when I get to know someone, I ask that individual to rate the following things in order of importance: beauty, intelligence and personality. I've had this same talk since middle school years. It was important for me to know why I was or was not liked. You see, I prefer not to be placed in a box or compared to anyone else. I am on my own little island, a ship sailing into the night of my life. I am more than just my looks, personality or intelligence. I frequently tell people that I am more than what meets the eyes. Sometimes we can be fooled by what we see. Yet I am full of layers, different versions of me not to be confined or defined by a few words or the opinions of others.

Furthermore, I discovered that being initially attracted to someone without seeing them physically first, and still seeing his or her potential is something special. This was a great feeling, and there was no physical intimacy of any sort. This was one of the best relationships I had ever experienced. We initially had to build the relationship during phone conversations and text messages because we couldn't always see each other due to our busy schedules. I have built a strong foundation of relationships not based on any superficial idea of what they should be. These relationships were special from the beginning because we did things differently which was probably better because we were interested in features other than the physical aspects.

This relationship wasn't about being with the most popular, the most beautiful or the finest by society's standards, and we had many conversations about various topics. We were happy with each other and didn't want each other to change. We brought out the best in each other and supported each other. Once we became more comfortable, we verbally expressed our feelings for each other. The things he shared were so sincere and heartfelt, I joked that he should save them for his vows.

The best relationships are those that encourage you to be yourself, nothing more and nothing less. There is value in being involved with people who love you despite your faults, flaws and failures… Even despite being imperfect, different, beautiful and not so beautiful. They accept you for who you are, and they don't try to change you. They just simply want to be with you and constantly speak into your life, as they want the best version of you. They realize that you can get better together, and they understand that building a relationship is a process. They see the caterpillar stage now, but they also know when the time is right, you will become that beautiful butterfly. A better version of you makes him or her want to be better. Sometimes you may get tired of meeting people and starting over again. It seems to be a cycle of love and lost, joy and pain, being in a relationship and then being alone. When you've loved and lost, you feel as though you cannot or will not love like this again. You begin to give up on the idea of love and being in love. And in one of your most vulnerable moments you meet that special someone, the yin to your yang, the one that makes you laugh out loud and smile again. The one that helps to remind you of your worth, your beauty and how special you are to others. The one that pushes you to greater heights and wants you to achieve your purpose and passion in life.

You know you've found the one when you realize that your life is complete. There will be days when things are not as we would like them to be, but when we keep God first in our lives and stay true to ourselves, everything will work out fine. Love conquers all, and in the end, true love will win. When you experience the true love of God, you realize that nothing or no one can come between that or take it away from you. We are free to be ourselves... No judging, just love, and understanding. You've found a love of your own, it feels good, and it feels right. Nothing compares to it, it is perfect for you and you cherish it. You love your life, the people in it, and you love yourself. Life is perfect for you right now.

CHAPTER 9

Transforming Light

"As we let our own light shine, we unconsciously give other people permission to do the same."
-Nelson Mandela

WE ARE ALL STARS in our own right and have gifts to share with the world. The world has become void of the light it once held many, many years ago. In a world that has become plagued with extreme darkness, hatred, social injustice and violence, we must be beacons of light and hope to others. We must allow our light to shine so that others can see the will of God working in us. Sometimes we are afraid to let our light shine within our relationship for various reasons. We often attempt to downplay ourselves by lessening our achievements, our skills or even our great potential.

We try to act normal when we are extraordinary human beings. Again, some people just have that *'It'* Factor... This thing that naturally attracts people to them. You don't really know what to call it, but there is just something about certain people. You cannot quite put your finger on it. People will recognize this thing about you. It is in your DNA, and it is a part of your personality, style and life. It is the anointing, the light of God shining on you.

There was a time I considered dimming my light for others. I thought it was shining too bright, and I did not want people to feel insecure or uneasy around me. The truth is, I wasn't really trying to do anything extra or special. I was just being myself. Looking back, I now realize this would not or could not continue. The thought was funny to me because stars shine bright. I mean that's why they were created. That's just what we do, and I say this in a non-bragging manner.

In Psalms 37:6, David reminds us that He (God) will make your righteousness shine like the noonday sun. In other words, He will make my light shine so bright that I cannot hide it even when wearing shades, glasses or any other form of disguise. Others are going to see right through it. God's glorious light is going to manifest itself in and through me. Nothing can dull my sparkle or dim my shine, unless I allow it. So, I have to stand in the mirror and encourage myself. I say to myself, "Go ahead girl with your bad self, you better shine bright like a diamond, like the star that you are." Even when I don't feel like shining so brightly, even when I considered dimming my light because others cannot handle it, even when I get tired, and even when I don't feel so beautiful, I know someone needs to see my sparkle. Because you see, this little light of mine, I am going to let it shine, let it shine, let it shine, let it shine.

My life's journey somewhat resembles the famous movie, The Wizard of Oz. You may know the story... In the beginning, Dorothy started out running away from her home in Kansas. She didn't want to be there because she believed she didn't belong anymore and was misunderstood by her loved ones. The tornado came and blew Dorothy away into 'Munchkin Land'. During the chaos of the tornado, the house fell onto the wicked witch of the east and killed her. Her sister, the wicked witch of the west, vows to seek revenge on Dorothy. The munchkins tell Dorothy that the wizard can help her get back home, so she eases on down that yellow brick road in search of the land of Oz. On this yellow brick road, she meets several individuals who all joined in her journey. She meets the scarecrow, the tin man and the cowardly lion.

You see, their journeys were all connected and intertwined with each other. They all lacked something in their lives, but little did they know, they needed someone to help them access it. They developed the right relationship with the right person at the right time. Just think about it. If Dorothy had not started her journey to get back home, she may not have met any of these characters. How many people had traveled down that same road and didn't pay attention to the scarecrow? How many people just thought the tin man was stuck in position? How many people laughed at the cowardly lion? Lions are considered the *king of the jungle*. He was just a big, scary cat. Yet once they joined forces, they were all stronger and better together.

After a long journey they finally reached their destination, the beautiful land of Oz. Then to add insult to injury, they were denied access to the wizard. However, they were not just going to accept no for an answer, especially after all they had gone through to get there. They had to sneak into the back door to see him. Now fast forward... The wizard attempts to send them on this impossible mission. Nevertheless, they accomplished this mission and returned to the wizard. In the end, everyone got exactly what they wanted and needed in their lives.

One of my favorite parts of the movie is towards the end when Dorothy realizes that she always had the power to go home. She already had what she needed, and it was the power inside of her. She didn't know it, and it took a long journey for her to realize it. Yet isn't this symbolic of life and how things happen? We search for this seemingly unattainable thing only to find out, it was there all along. We already have exactly what we need in our lives. I really love this movie, but the funny part is this. She ended up right back in the very same place from which she tried to escape. That's the circle of life. We move through life and go down different paths, but life brings us back exactly where we were meant at the destined time.

In the beginning of this book, I spoke of how I loved to read, write and speak as a child. As I write this book, I am brought back to that tender age of about eight or nine years old when I first started journaling about my life experiences. I am returning to 2nd Sundays for our Youth Sunday Program at Payne Memorial AME Church. I am reminded of participating in plays and productions at Holy Ghost Catholic School and Xavier Preparatory High School. I am also brought back to those moments of being on the stage at the City of Love Church, whether I was ministering through theatrical arts, mime or speaking. Presently, I am speaking at churches, conferences and conventions all over the world.

Remember we must have faith and see it spiritually before it manifests itself in the physical world.

So here we are, back where we started. I am still a work in progress, still on my spiritual journey and still discovering Teriece Cherell. This is my journey to Teriece Cherell, and I thank you for allowing me to share it with you. You are welcome into my world. Now you are free to go forth on your own journey to discover you. Relationships are the greatest blessings and lessons teaching us about life. These various relationships contribute to our overall health, wealth, success and growth as individuals.

There is nothing more beautiful or greater than an open, loving heart. When our hearts are open, we can both give and receive that pure unadulterated, unconditional love of God. For God is love, and since we are made in His image and likeness, we too are love. With open hearts, hands and minds, we can begin to experience the fullness of God and live our best lives. I encourage you to keep living, learning and loving on this journey.

My heart has been opened to you,
Teriece Cherell

Transforming Light

-A letter from Danika Louis Kennedy

The light of the body is the eye: if therefore thine eye be single; thy whole body shall be full of light. The eye is the lamp of the body. If your vision is clear, your whole body will be full of light. Your eyes are a window for your body. When they are good, you have all the light you need.
-Matthew 6:22

FIRST IMPRESSIONS ARE said to last the longest. While I've found that to be mostly true, this was not the case with Ms. Teriece Reynolds. I met Teriece on a fall afternoon in September as she interviewed for a job with my employer. My first impression of her was that she was very mysterious and rather bashful. Coming highly recommended based on her work ethic and ability to get any job done, I was excited about the opportunity to meet my possible future colleague. Teriece nervously walked into my office and began to tell me a little bit about herself. As she modestly spoke of her past work experiences and her involvement with her church, I could not help but notice that she would close her eyes as she spoke about the church and her darling little 'Rooda-Tooda' (two things she was so passionate about). The interview went well, but I walked away from the interview a little puzzled. As I contemplated my decision on whether we should hire Teriece, I concluded that I did indeed want to hire her because I wanted to know more about this highly recommended, seemingly shy, God-fearing woman who impressed me with her superior articulation and ability to "get any job done".

Teriece did not disappoint! Her first few weeks of work, she picked up on things that had taken some other individuals' months to grasp. However, I was still baffled by the closing of her eyes when she spoke of her work with the church, but I never brought it up to her. I then noticed that Teriece had a plethora of sunglasses as she wore a different pair nearly three times a week. I did eventually joke with her about the number of pairs of sunglasses I would see her wearing. She then told me about "Hollywood"! That made perfect sense, but I was still confused about the closing of the eyes when she spoke about her 'Rooda-Tooda' and The City of Love.

As I reflected upon Teriece as an individual, through the scripture, an epiphany was revealed. Teriece has protected/closed her eyes throughout her journey because she has been focused on so much more than worldly things. Her eyes are truly the lamp of her body. Her vision is clear and her whole body is full of light. So, I say to you, "Keep your eyes protected! Protect your lamp! God is doing a mighty thing with you, and I am blessed to have you in my presence.

-Danika

www.ingramcontent.com/pod-product-compliance
Lightning Source LLC
LaVergne TN
LVHW020644100826
845148LV00012B/2334

* 9 7 8 0 5 7 8 2 1 4 3 9 9 *